DATE DUE			
JAN 1 8 '01			
JUN 2 7 '01			
MAR 4 '03			
NOV 3 0 2004			

Fire from the Dragon's Tongue

Essays about Living with Nature in the Siskiyou Mountains

Diana Coogle

Laughing Dog Press
Blue Ridge, Georgia

These essays were first broadcast on Jefferson Public Radio,
Ashland, Oregon.

"Autumn in Chiaroscuro Tints" was first printed
in *West Wind Review* under the title "Autumn Browns."

"The Ecological Continuum of the Forest" was first printed
in *The Trumpeter, A Journal of Ecosophy.*

I wish to express my gratitude to my sister Sharon Coogle,
who bolstered me up when frustration knocked me down
and provided invaluable artistic direction besides;

to Denise Maas and Wendy Huber at Rogue Community College
for computer expertise in times of dire need;

to Lucy Edwards, Paul Westhelle, and John Baxter
at Jefferson Public Radio and to Tom Olbrich, formerly at JPR,
for their help and continuing friendship;

and to Lenor Chappell, Amy Belkin,
and Melinda Haldeman, for their careful edits.

Laughing Dog Press
Blue Ridge, Georgia 30513
*
9700 Thompson Creek Road
Applegate, OR 97530
dcoogle@rogue.cc.or.us

❖

Cover design by Sharon Coogle
Photograph of author by Ela Lamblin
This book was set in Times, 10 point.

For **MY MOTHER AND FATHER**

*The excitement of life is in the numinous experience
wherein we are given to each other in that larger
celebration of existence in which all things attain
their highest expression, for the universe,
by definition, is a single gorgeous celebratory event.*

Thomas Berry
The Dream of the Earth

Contents

Giving Plants and Animals Their Due

Living with Nature

Foreword

by

John Baxter, Director of New Media
Jefferson Public Radio

In the early 1980s, Diana Coogle's commentaries began airing weekly on Jefferson Public Radio's flagship station, KSOR. When she pitched the idea to me, I instantly recognized that the commentaries would speak to our listeners' experiences. They were very much about living in the mythical "State of Jefferson," the mountainous region of Southern Oregon and Northern California consisting of the Klamath, Rogue, and Umpqua basins and their associated coastal streams. To those who call this region "home," it is a place valued for its stunning natural beauty, sense of community, and fierce independent spirit. Reverence for these attributes has always been present in Diana's writing.

Diana's commentaries focused on her experiences as a single mother living in the mountains above the Applegate Valley in southwestern Oregon. Not only did they resonate with many KSOR listeners, who, like Diana, were intimately acquainted with the rigors of rural life, but the commentaries won fans among our "urban" population who didn't have to walk up a hill to get to their homes and whose bathtubs, unlike Diana's, were usually inside their homes. Soon listeners realized that Diana's commentaries described more than rural living, and they followed her through her travels away from the Applegate and through the joys and the travails of being a single mother in the '80s. Nearly twenty years later, they still follow her on Jefferson Public Radio.

One of the limitations of radio as a way to communicate with people is that ideas broadcast are here one moment in time and gone just as fast - programming on radio simply does not adjust well to people's busy lives. In that vein, it is great to have Diana's writing bound and portable, so that you can grab a good cup of coffee or tea and experience what Jefferson Public Radio listeners have experienced for so many years.

Ashland, Oregon
October 1998

Introduction

"What is needed on our part," says Thomas Berry in *The Dream of the Earth*, "is the capacity for listening to what the earth is telling us."

I live where I do - in a remote spot in the Siskiyou Mountains of southern Oregon - in the hopes of developing that capacity for listening to the earth. I built my house in 1974 on a steep mountainside above the Applegate valley. My son, Ela, was two years old then and lived with me until he went to college at age seventeen (except for the every-other-year he was with his father just over the mountain). It was a good place for learning to listen to the earth; no houses, roads, cars, or other signs of people were visible from the house; no electricity brought appliances and motors here. I heated with wood, cooked with propane, lit the dark house with kerosene lamps, bathed in an outdoor shower, and used an outhouse for a toilet. All these things are still true, and if I also have a telephone now, it's because I thought that listening to the human world might be important, too, and if I have a car as well, at least it can't be driven any closer than a five-minute walk up the hill and through the woods to the house, and if I have a generator to run my computer and sewing machine, I acknowledge its necessity and hasten to add that it's very small and not too noisy. I want to listen to the earth.

I listen to the earth in all its seasons. I have heard the incessant rain of long winters drumming on my tin roof, and I have heard the cold snap in the air. I have listened to the earth through the running water under my canoe and in the beat of my hiking boots on the mountain trail. I have listened to scorpions and spiders, to deer and owls, to mushrooms and salmon; I have had my exchanges of temper with dogs and skunks and poison oak. I have listened to the thin distant song of the stars and tried to understand the stories in the rocks. I have eaten herbs and apples from the good earth to listen through my teeth; I have listened through my hands on soft mosses and papery madrone bark. Through all my senses I listen.

From that listening have come these essays. They assume knowledge of my living conditions, mentioned above, and of my son, who now lives in Seattle. They draw on my adventures in the wilderness areas of the Klamath-Siskiyou Mountains and on the natural environment of my home, the essential setting in which I play my guitar and practice my yoga, cook, garden, take long walks, pet my cats, read good books, and write the tales I hear as I listen to the world around me.

Keeping Pace with the Seasons

If Eskimos Have Forty Words for Snow, What Do Oregonians Call Rain?

A very light rain that draws a belly-dancer's veil over the moon and gossamer curtains over the mountain is called a mist.

A mist that thickens and congeals until it has swallowed moon, mountain, fenceposts, trees, and the hand in front of your face is called fog.

Rain that dots and dashes against the house like a stuttering Morse code but that barely puts a dew-drops-on-a-spider-web gleam on your hair when you go outside is called precipitation. An accumulation of such a rain is called measurable precipitation.

Rain with sun shining through it is called "the time when foxes have weddings."

When you feel a few drops of rain on your head and are just beginning to wish you'd brought your umbrella and then wonder if it's raining, after all, you would say, "It's just sprinkling."

A rain that falls slowly and steadily with more space between drops than substance in the thing itself is called a drizzle, but if it throws itself down with a vengeance and then suddenly gives up with a laugh, it's called a shower.

The rain that fights with itself, spitting and spluttering, knocking your hat off and driving into your face with tooth and claw, is called "raining cats and dogs."

If the rain falls evenly, as though poured through a sprinkling can, it's called a good, hard rain. The good, hard rain that gushes down like out of a bucket is called "pouring buckets," as in, "It's absolutely pouring buckets out there!" Another term for this kind of rain is a downpour, and if it washes great mud slides of the mountain into the valley and sets the creeks to a thunderous roar, it's called a torrential downpour.

A rain preceded by flashing snatches of lightning, crashing catastrophes of thunder, and smashing calamities of wind is called a storm. If the winds uproot trees and rip off roofs with a leviathan temper, what you have is a tempest. It is best to keep the top on your teapot during a tempest.

A rain that comes down in solid sheets for more than two days and two nights is called a deluge. If it goes on for forty days and forty nights, it's a flood.

Very cold rain that stings with sharp, hot-needle stabs is called sleet.

Cold rain that falls in big, white drops of lace antimacassars is called snow.

A rain that awakens bright tulips and sunny daffodils with every splashing warm drop is an April shower, but the winter rain that bombards the mountain with cataracts and waterfalls is such that we would say, with Chaucer, "Lord this is huge rayn./This were a weder for to slepen inne!"

And the Rain It Rains

Firs shimmer with raindrops. Fog rises from the valley, swallowing the mountain from the bottom up, then sinks, regurgitating the mountain, a gray-green bubble encircled by a white smoke ring. Day after day, the sky is a study in variations of gray. If an occasional spot of blue comes shockingly forth, it is quickly hushed by its prudish, solemn, serious neighbors in gray. We'll have no gaiety here, they admonish, pulling Puritan skirts over lacy petticoats.

Rain like a wet, gray sponge wraps around the mountain. It rains all night and half the day; then the rest of the day gives up and goes to bed, hungover, heavy and gray.

The day droops. Gravity is stronger than usual, pulling all objects heavily towards the center of the earth; the gray sky looms close overhead, pushing down. The rain comes down; fir branches press down; even the long aluminum tubes of the wind chimes press towards the earth. All lines press down.

Heavy skies can be monotonous and oppressive. San Francisco holds the record for suicides. Italians in their Mediterranean climate have hot tempers, but the English sense of humor is dour and dry, in contrast to the English weather, which is dour and wet. The French word for weather is the same as the word for time - *le temps*. *Par tous les temps* means in all weather, but it must originally have meant through all sorts of times - good times, bad times, sunny times, stormy times.

If the skies are gray, we must create our own sunny time. If the pull of rain and the pressure of sky would seem to drive us into the wet sponge of the earth, we can still take advantage of our inner environment. Inside the house, which has its own atmosphere and air flow, the downward pressure of heavy weather is irrelevant. At night, in the house, the rain is known only by sound, and in contrast to the insistent downward pull of visual rain, this audible rain is lively and irregular, a dance to relieve monotony. Now is the time and now is the weather to make a cup of tea and sit in a comfortable place with a good book, to stay cozy and warm and travel to distant places and

5

times - to a Moroccan harem, to the early American west with Lewis and Clark, to the top of Mt. Everest, to the Blue Ridge Mountains during the Civil War, to the Atlantic Ocean in the perfect storm. And then one looks up, notices the rain, listens, gets up to stretch, walk, refill the tea, restoke the fire, and then resettle with the book to travel again, cozy in the assurance of resisting the downward pull of a month of rain.

Winter Survival Tips

For two months winter has played an endless fugue with rain, clouds, and gray skies. If your inner child is peevish and petulant, if you feel yourself slipping into winter doldrums, hold on! Don't give in! Arm yourself with these winter survival tips:

(1) Refuse to succumb to the dominant paradigm that grey equals gloom. Make a study of the sky, and you'll find a plethora of variations on gray clouds - they're striped and brindled, splotched and rippled, distinctly layered or seamlessly smeared in a watercolor wash, white to dark and a thousand shades in between. Find new words for gray - platinum, pearl, steel, taupe, but stay away from dirty words - ash, charcoal, smoke.

(2) Never elevate your hopes. Just because you see stars at 9:00 p.m. doesn't mean you'll see sunshine tomorrow; just because the eastern sky is clear at 8:00 in the morning doesn't mean those sweeping gray clouds from the south won't obliterate the blue by noon. Each time you leave survival mode, you are in danger of slipping deeper into doldrums, and with each slip you'll have a harder time regaining good humor. Take any slice of pale blue sky, any glimpse of well-focused moon as a gift. Savor it, enjoy it, and remind your inner child that it's not polite to ask for more than is given.

(3) Make the indoors bright and cheerful. Keep the house clean; depression has no better friend than disorder and dirt. Indulge the senses. Simmer luscious stews on top of the stove, and bake often not only because baking emits good smells and leads to pleased palates, but also because a hot oven warms the house the way a good hug warms the heart.

(4) Use escape items. Books or movies can lift you out of foul weather, whereas other escapes don't so much remove you from winter as remove winter from your spirit. You can't be glum if you're making notecards for a friend or if you've lost yourself in working out the intricacies of a Bach sarabande on the guitar. You could be immersed for hours, well out of reach of the wet enstranglement of

winter, but it's also a delicious feeling to return to the moment, listen to the tap-dance on the roof, and be glad you're here, now, in this Oregon, in this winter.

(5) Enjoy it! Walk in it; notice its details. Rain shimmers as it drones down; the raindrum plays polyrhythms on leaves, roof, earth. Mists veil and then reveal mountains; little round clouds are nosed about by hummocks like balls tossed by seals. Relish the sponginess of the earth as you walk. Winter is full of sensualities. Don't miss them!

(6) Keep heart. Just as surely as the planet turns around the sun, winter turns to spring. It has never been otherwise.

Ice Stub Appendages

Having lived in my little house on the mountain for more than a quarter century, I have learned many tricks for surviving Oregon winters - carrying rubber boots in my car in case it snows while I'm in town and I have to walk a half mile up the hill from the paved road to get home; stoking the fire at night so I'll have hot coals when I wake up in the morning; putting kerosene lamps in front of mirrors to double my light during long winter evenings. But it seems there has been no trick to solve the problem of cold feet.

Like stubs of ice on the ends of my legs, my feet never warm up, no matter the layers of blankets, no matter the thickness of socks. In vain, I put on my warmest insulated REI socks before I go to bed; they only keep the cold in. In vain, I beg my two cats to warm my feet by curling over them; the cats prefer the warmer places about my body. In vain, I place the cold foot of one leg behind the warm knee of the other and vise versa; then I have two cold knees as well as two cold feet.

Last summer I discovered that peppermint foot cream encases the foot in a warm glow, so on the first cold night of the winter, thinking gleefully I had outwitted the Demon of Cold Feet at last, I massaged peppermint foot cream into my cold feet and crawled into bed. But my feet stayed cold. Peppermint foot cream, like socks, only works if the feet are already warm.

It does work to warm up my socks by laying them directly on the wood-burning stove, but, besides the fact that it's easy to burn a hole in my socks that way, the truth is, I don't like to sleep in socks and always wake up in the middle of the night to pull them off. And the point is, isn't it, to sleep uninterrupted?

I have also had some limited success with a hot-water bottle. That works if I keep moving it around my feet, but that's a lot of attention to give when I want to go to sleep, and if I don't remember to take the hot-water bottle out of the bed before I fall asleep, I wake up in the night with a cold glob of rubber at my feet.

I know about electric blankets, but mine is a non-electric house, and, anyway, I detest electric blankets. Once when I was a child, I spent the night with a friend who generously offered me the bed with the electric blanket but pointed out that if I wet the bed, I would be electrocuted. Even though I was many years past wetting the bed, the thought of what would happen if I did terrified me, and what if I drooled or my eyes watered? My friend slept with the electric blanket; I slept with cold feet. Anyway, I have always liked the weight and spreading warmth of good wool blankets on a cold winter night. But under the blankets my feet, like abandoned children, weep with cold.

This winter, though, I think maybe I've found the solution - an old-fashioned bedwarmer. This practical device has long handles on two round metal disks scooped out like saucers. Every evening just before bed, I fill this hollow with glowing orange coals from the wood-burning stove. It's so hot I'm afraid it'll burn the sheets if I leave it in the bed like a hot-water bottle, so I spend a few minutes in the ritual of sliding the hot bedwarmer all over the cold sheets, letting it linger longest where the feet lie. The sheets retain the heat while I empty the coals back into the fire and blow out the kerosene lamps, and when I return, I slip into a bed as welcoming as sunshine after a cold swim. My feet snuggle into a cocoon that radiates a lasting warmth into my feet. No longer a warm body with ice stub appendages, I stretch out luxuriously full length in the bed. I smile, warm all over, and slip into an uninterrupted winter's sleep.

What To Wear
When the Weather Turns Cold

Occasionally on a cold winter day I'll see someone in town wearing shorts. It's a pitiful sight. My friend Leah says these people are from Alaska and wear shorts in winter because the weather we call cold is warm to them. My theory is that such people come from southern California and jump into the same everyday costume every day because they don't understand what winter is for.

If I wear shorts in January, when can I wear my beautiful wool sweaters, the soft, deep purple one with its folds of wool at the neck, or the thick grey Scandinavian sweater Maren gave me in Sweden? In these sweaters I feel snug and secure, as though winter doldrums can't reach me inside such warmth.

It's only in winter that I can wear my black leather gloves with sheepskin on the inside, so warm and soft; my little pointed-toe elf boots, and the velvet, Renaissance-style hats I make with Seminole patchwork bands. It's only in winter that I can wrap myself in my swirling, full-length grey wool cloak, so flamboyant in style, subdued in color. I paid $40 for it in a used clothing store. When I asked my sister if I had been a fool to buy it, she said I would have been a fool not to, so now I feel not only dashing and dramatic in my cloak but wise as well. But wouldn't I look ridiculous in my elf boots, velvet hat, flowing wool cloak, and shorts!

Because we wear more clothes in winter, we have a chance to play with more combinations. I can emphasize color: a turquoise shirt with my purple velvet skirt and the bold touch of my deep rose hat; a blue leotard with a maroon skirt and a rose-and-blue-striped cardigan, a black scarf with splotches of rose, and the black hat with a blue band. In winter I can wear long skirts, luxurious and homey at the same time, with various shirts, vests, jackets, and sweaters. I can wear my black rayon skirt, blotched with bright bouquets of blue, red, and yellow flowers, and sling my sky-blue silk scarf over my shoulders. I can't wear this scarf in the summer, when it feels hot and limpid around my neck, but in the winter it has the warm softness of a cat in my lap.

There is much pleasure in clothes - their textures: the rayons and velvets that glide and swirl, the silks that flow like water, the warm wools that wrap us in coziness and cheer our hearts like a warm kiss; their colors: rich or soft, deep or light, lively or gentle; their surprises of new combinations; their bright or subtle patterns: drooping and skipping rosettes that flounce with every step, stripes that rise and ripple just for being taken for a walk; the hats and scarves and big, dramatic cloaks. Wouldn't it be a pity never to experience these clothes? Indeed, I do pity those who wear shorts in the winter. They just don't understand what winter is for.

Paean to Cold

I like these cold days and cold, cold nights. The water to the house has already frozen, so I don't have to worry about the pipes freezing, and a walk to the creek for water has become a daily ritual. Except I'm afraid some spiteful god would hear me and take away my plumbing permanently, I would admit I like the walk up the creek on frosty-crisp days; I like to dip my buckets into pools of forest-dark water; I like the weight of the buckets lengthening my arms as I slip through the woods back to the house. It's an elemental reminder, this pouring water from buckets I filled at the creek, like putting a new log on the fire in the stove.

I like the change of sounds in the cold, too. The silence of a night in the grip of hard frost is a suspension of sound, like the breathless moment at the end of a concert that was so beautiful the audience can't bear to break the spell with the clatter of applause. In that hollow stillness the music still lingers; in the hollow stillness of sharp, cold nights, when the stars glitter like welding sparks through the skylights over my bed, the air is filled with a suspension of unheard winter-night sounds - the wind that isn't blowing, the frozen leaves that aren't rustling, the water that no longer gurgles through the faucet. In a moment, when I can bear to, I'll break the silence with my applause.

In late December, 1990, I experienced the coldest weather I've ever known. My son, Ela, was home from college for the holidays. One night he, a friend, and I stayed up past midnight, and Ela, with his unrelenting energy that knows no boundaries of dark or cold or lateness of hour, suggested a walk. We bundled in our winter coats and hats, pulled on gloves and boots, and left the house.

The night was brittle with cold. A newly waning moon cut a hole in the sky, to which I quoted aloud from Robinson Jeffers, "No eye but that misformed one, the moon's past fullness." The snow glittered with tiny, hard drops of spilled stars wherever that eye glanced. The snow crunched and squeaked beneath our boots; each step broke diamonds. The hard liquid whiteness from the black sky, streaming down wherever the old logging road made an opening for it through the coffee-black forest, blended with the solid white hardness on the earth. The cold snapped in the air like lightning.

"How cold do you think it is?" I wondered aloud as we stopped at the frozen creek. Chris looked at the thermometer on his new watch.

"Seven below zero," he said.

Sparklingly cold! Bitterly cold, to those inclined towards bitterness, which I'm not.

Ela's bullroarer, swinging fast over his head, wailed with a wild, unworldly moan intensified and sharpened by the cold. With that wail and in that intense beauty, which, like music, had to be given up at the same moment it was taken in, I felt the despair of Gerard Manley Hopkins:

> *How to keep - is there any any, is there none such,*
> *nowhere known some, bow or brooch or*
> *braid or brace, lace, latch or catch or key*
> *to keep*
> *Back beauty, keep it, beauty, beauty, beauty...from*
> *vanishing away?*

Then the golden echo of Hopkins' answer floated to me through the night: "Give beauty back, beauty, beauty, beauty, back to God, beauty's self and beauty's giver."

And a god is surely there in such cold winter scenes, spilling beauty everywhere, but I am as much in despair of knowing how to return it to this god as I am of keeping it from vanishing away.

14

Cross-country Skiing by Moonlight

My boots were firmly snapped into my skis and my poles already dangling from my wrists as I waited for the others in our party to finish their endless preparations out of trunks of cars and back ends of pick-ups. Finally Joe said, "Are we ready?" and he and I shoved our poles into the hard-packed snow and took off around the side of Mt. Ashland, followed by the others. Fourteen skiers soon became a broken line of twos, threes, and fours; our banter became whispers, then silence.

Dark was pushing the red-streaked sunset down the horizon, and the queen of the night had just risen full and large, reflecting on the broad slopes of snow. The unbroken whiteness of the bulk of the mountain rose to my right; the open blackness of space where the mountain dropped into the night sank to my left. It was a black and white world. The white orb in the black sky threw the hidden sun's light, alchemically changed, back to earth, to this white glove over the earth, these fields of white cold that reflected light back into the surrounding dark, giving us so much cold white light that visibility was not a problem. We could see forever, and what there was to see was white snow with splotches of black that I knew were trees and a black sky with a large white bulb of a moon.

The three or four of us in the lead, far ahead of the other skiers, stopped for a breather under the shelter of a lightning-broken fir tree. Skiing, I had been warm, sweating under my jacket; still, I felt the bite of the wind, the sharp teeth of the night air, the cold of the moonlight. Davey skied up to us and, acting as our St. Bernard, opened his pack, and passed around a flask of brandy. The brandy had a bite, like the wind, but it was the bite of fire, not ice. I took chocolates out of my pack and passed them around, and the chocolate, hard with cold, cracked and melted thick and sweet and as smooth as snow in our mouths. Then with a glance and a nod, we shoved our poles into the hard snow and took off again.

Ahead was a long, icy downhill slope. Kurt skied it first. "That looks tricky," Joe murmured, then took off gamely. I was next. Once I started there would be no stopping till I reached the far end. I took a deep breath and pushed off gently. The icy surface, the cold glare of the moon, the blinding reflection off the snow, the unstoppable momentum, the slide, the difficulty of balance - the cold air slicing through my lungs, the wind at the back of my neck.... Concentrate, I told myself. Balance. Hang onto the moon. Watch for black dots that might be rocks. Keep the skis pointed forward, tips up. Balance. And then I was there, skiing to a not graceful but at least upright and exultant stop beside Joe and Kurt, and we turned to watch the others, black lines and dots slashing across the white hillside like living calligraphy scrawled by the moon across the blank page of the snow.

Soon we had all made it to the hut that was our destination. In it were two tables and no chairs, and everything seemed wet and dirty, but since Davey had heroically carried firewood in his backpack, adding pounds and pounds to his weight, we soon had a fire popping, and with that and the room filling with boisterous people, dinginess receded. And the hosts of this birthday party had not forgotten their birthday duties. Out came the cake; out came the whipped cream - which had sprayed itself empty inside Helen's pack. Katarina brought out thermoses of hot coffee well laced with Kahlua and poured us all gut-warming, heart-warming drinks. We sang happy birthday to Joe, ate Katarina's amazing carrot cake, drank our intoxicating coffee (intoxication that would be both enhanced and eradicated once we hit the outdoors again), gradually unzipped our jackets, and warmed our vocal cords telling about this fall and that one, the effects of the moon, the soreness in our legs.

The way back was a gentle downhill, but it was again push, glide, push through a black-and-white world muted now by a thin blanket of clouds, until before we knew it, it was the glare of electric lights in a Jacksonville restaurant with the hot cheese-and-tomato smell of fresh pizza steaming before us and the slap of color assaulting us everywhere - in clothes, on walls, chairs, tablecloths. That other world was behind us, something to talk about now - the difficulty of the traverse, the falls we took, the disaster of the whipped cream, the surprise of the Kahlua in the coffee, the birthday cake - something remote already, an unreal world of sharpness of breath and hardness of ice, of gleam of moon and brightness of snow, an unreal world of black and white that had been pinched off like a fistful of clay from the larger mold of our lives and left to sit on inner altars, the shrines to unforgettable experiences.

16

Theme-based Flower Beds

In these early spring months your impulse might be to get out in the garden and plant, plant, plant. But such precipitous action now might cause regrets later when you gaze on a disorderly array of badly placed flowers growing in floral communities of spiteful neighbors that have turned your peaceful garden into a snarly mess. For a garden of beauty and harmony in July, it's best to take some time for planning now. Although gardening books often suggest organizing flower beds according to color, height, preference of sun or shade, and so forth, I've found that flower beds are best arranged by theme. For spectacular results from your flowers this summer, plant according to the following plans:

The Romantic Bed: Black-eyed Susan goes in first, and next to it sweet William. Johnny Jump-ups running side by side with sweet William make a nice contrast, but unless you want to bother with bleeding hearts and Job's tears, plant some Rosemary next to the Johnny Jump-ups and let sweet William continue down the path alone with black-eyed Susan. Next plant a batch of candytuft, surrounded by love-in-a-mist. This theme can be repeated until you are ready to throw in some impatiens, after which it's a good idea to put in a big Jack-in-the-pulpit. Then plant lots of passion flower and, close by, a blanket flower. Lastly, plant a beautiful soft display of baby's breath. (I prefer not to add twinflower here, but that is a possibility.)

If you still have room, you should consider continuing this bed with the following: broom and cup-and-saucer vine, milkweed and buttercup, thimbleberry and a pincushion flower, money plant and a good, full bank of thrift. Floss flower should now be added next to honeysuckle. There should be plenty of thyme but no rue. It would be good to keep a passion flower here and there, and at the very end of the row, plant bearded iris, angelica, and forget-me-not.

The Religious Bed: Monkshood and St. John's wort look good focused around a Madonna lily. Angel's trumpet should arch above, interspersed with the beautiful bird of paradise. This is the bed for pasqueflower and Michaelmas daisy, and you should encircle the entire bed, of course, with everlasting. A statue of St. Francis of Assisi looks very nice here.

The Garden of Eden Bed: Keep canarybird vine at the greatest possible distance from catnip, spider flower from toadflax, and lamb's ear from dandelion. Bee balm and butterfly bush can go just about anywhere. Place your kingfisher daisy by water, monkey flower close to trees, foxglove at the edge of the woods, and horseradish in the meadows.

Day and Night Bed: The circular day bed should have one large sunflower, surrounded by, progressively, morning glory, day lily, and four o'clocks. The night bed should have one large moonvine surrounded by spangles of starflowers, asters, and star jasmine. The whole should be connected by an intertwined infinity symbol of cosmos.

The Literary Bed: The fairy tale section will grow lushly with any of the following combinations: a fairy wand between maiden's wreath and toadflax; Jacob's ladder leading up maidenhair fern to Queen Anne's lace (or princess flower); pot-of-gold correopsis at the end of an arching row of rainbow-splash petunias; lady's slipper with pumpkin; witch hazel with scotch broom; snapdragon followed by spearmint and bloodroot. The Medieval section is very showy with Canterbury bells for Chaucer and sword fern and touch-me-not between two large bursts of passion flower for Tristan and Isolde. For the poetry section try bells of Ireland for Yeats, a host of golden daffodils for Wordsworth, and the daffodil called *poetica narcissus* for our contemporary poets. Shakespeare would be well represented by globe amaranth (a real stage-setter in the garden). Also, if you set love-lies-bleeding, lady's mantle, and the lion's beard buttercup adjacent to one another, you have a nice little representation of *Romeo and Juliet*. Lily of the Nile also suggests Shakespeare, since the lily of the Nile is surely the lady of the Nile, which is surely Cleopatra, but if you're going to include Cleopatra, you'll probably also have to plant a Madonna lily here, thinking not of the Madonna of the Religious Bed but of that other, more modern Madonna, next to which you would certainly plant that belladonna lily called naked lady. It might be best to separate lily of the Nile and Madonna lily with the harmonizing effects of a bugle flower and a trumpet vine, but never with a red hot poker. Use painted tongue for a border in this bed.

Put a bench under a tree for long afternoons of summer reading in your garden. The enjoyment you'll reap from your book will be doubled by the blossoms and perfumes of your flower beds.

Every Good Hike Ends with a Swim

I love the wilderness, I love to hike, and I love to swim. When I was invited on a hike-and-raft trip into the proposed Rogue-Illinois Wild Rivers National Park, I didn't have to think twice about accepting. The weather was unprecedentedly hot for May, but hiking in 100-degree heat isn't so bad with backpacks on horses and good swimming along the way. Lunch on Indigo Creek was a refreshing break. After that, the trail charged more steeply upward, and the afternoon air hung hot in the forest, but the vision of diving into cool green campsite waters upheld me.

Assumptions, like illusions, will sustain us for a long time - for as long as we believe they're real. Four miles into the wilderness and already committed, I was informed there was no swimming hole, no creek, no river, no body of water at the end of this hike. I felt cheated. I wanted to turn around and go back. I couldn't believe that David Atkin, leader and organizer of this trip into the north Kalmiopsis, had planned to take this group of state-wide conservation leaders up this strenuous mountain without even providing a swim at the end. Complaints poured out with the sweat - how hot it was, how arduous the climb, how thirsty I was. If David's plan had been to convince us to make this area a national park, his plan was backfiring. When it was an abstract idea, I had thought it a good one. Now, in the arduous reality, I wasn't so sure, not just because it was a difficult climb that only the strong few would attempt but also because, though beautiful, it was not Yosemite-spectacular. So what was the point?

It had come down to "first one foot, then the other." I had ceased to look at the surrounding woods, ceased to hear the surrounding birdcall, ceased to notice the masses of wildflowers - all I could see was my foot on the trail, and all I could think of was water. Dehydrated and dizzy, I squeezed my plastic canteen for the last few drops of warm water to share with my hiking companions. First one foot, then the other, as dreams of water bubbled in my ears and teased my throat.

A call came from the hiker above: "I hear water!"

"An illusion," I muttered, stumbling on. "An audial mirage."

But, no, it was water, a tiny stream splashing through a rocky crack in the midst of ferns and mosses and thickets of willows and carpets of flowers - real water, for drinking if not for swimming. I drank a quart, a power potion. A new woman, I started upward again, and the beauty and life of the forest came back into focus: the rattlesnake curling under the oak bush, the pileated woodpecker pounding at his fir snag, the pair of western tanagers flirting across the trail, the king snake scuttling through the salal, the wedge-shaped, fern-and-flower meadows yielding slow-shutter-speed glimpses of misted mountains. The air, though hot, was clean and clear, and the trees - "A brotherhood of venerable trees," Wordsworth said, and I here among them.

And then with one step I was out of the forest, and spread before me like the dance floor in a chandelier-lit hall was Silver Prairie, an immense expanse of meadow sloping in long steps towards the curve of its center and pointing like an arrow south into the Kalmiopsis. The chandelier-like light was sunshine and blue skies and glimmering ridges of mountains. My god, it was something! Bubbling mountains, the sloping meadow, the pinpointed placement of firs deep in its right side, the open blue sky after the closeness of the forest, the pyramidal point of Bald Mountain in the vista of peaks - Yosemite-spectacular.

It was Thoreau who told us that in order to preserve the world, we must keep our wildness, a truth I learned again in Silver Prairie. David Atkin had not been wrong. Without a word, with only a gesture, he had made his point. I understood why people had lain in front of bulldozers to prevent a road on Bald Mountain. I couldn't get enough of nature. I was swimming not in water but in prairie and sky and mountains, diving into chasms of land and of life lost in the steepness before me. I pitched my tent on one of the flat steps leading to the concave center of Silver Prairie and swam for hours. Under a sparkling Scorpio I slept and at dawn awoke again to this harmony of mountains. I raised my cup of fresh spring water to the mountains and the sky in a silent toast and prayer: "Here's to the new Rogue-Illinois Wild Rivers National Park. May its wildness live forever to be the preservation of our world. A sante and amen."

Waterloo on the Illinois River

Where Silver Creek charges into the Illinois River, the river thrashes turbulent, silver-tipped and emerald in the rapids. On the opposite shore of that violence lay a man nakedly catering to the sun. Because I knew that man could only have gotten there by swimming the river, I knew the river could be swum, and I was seized with a desire to swim the river myself. Because it looked impassable and I knew it wasn't, I wanted to defeat the river, to conquer it, and to master it. Once I tried, and in defeat analyzed the necessity of more assertion against the current, so twice I tried, and the second time more nearly succeeded. The third time I swam behind the man who had done it already, watched carefully the course he took, and threw myself into the rapids after him.

The water was churning with its own energy and force, its own will. My will to the river was as a piece of straw to the wind. I was turned and churned, twisted, corkscrewed, pulled, pushed, and bashed till I didn't know where water was and where air, and if I did, couldn't get to the one I needed. There was a moment of real fright, but, remembering that panic kills, I remembered, too, to trust to the river, and so I did, and the river carried me, none too gently, and spat me out, ignominious in defeat, on the familiar shore. Panting, worn out, I crawled to a rock to soothe my battered ego.

So the Illinois River became my Waterloo, but only for the moment. Defeated but not down, I climbed into the raft for the journey downstream and gave myself to the river for the rest of the day. As it is a particularly green and beautiful, deep and pure river, I was soon out of the raft and in the water again. With gentle, easy strokes I glided downstream with the now lazily moving current. The river here was friendly and peaceful, compatible. I rolled onto my back and sculled gently, watching the osprey in the air above me. Master of my movements in the water, I was a swimmer again, a mermaid, a fish, an otter, a water creature of a new and unknown species.

I pulled myself onto the raft in order to dive deeply into the river. "Can you dive to the bottom?" challenged my friend who had swum the river at Silver Creek. Without a word, I dived in and went down and down until, still far from the bottom, my lungs hurt for air. But my friend was still going down and down and down until he disappeared in the water the way an airplane disappears while you watch it in the sky. At last he came up and tossed me a stone from the bottom. Agape, I asked him how deep it was.

"Forty feet," he said as he pulled himself onto the raft.

Forty feet? The river had defeated me again - too big, too deep, too swift. I could neither swim across it nor touch its bottom. And yet, as I continued down the river, dancing in its riverside waterfalls, dappling in its deeper, stiller moments, crashing through its rapids on the raft, I was glad the Illinois River was the master of me. With the challenges met but not won, I felt the proper respect and awe for the river. It was bigger than I. I had forced nothing on it; graciously it had accepted me and given me of itself. I had not been defeated by the river but given to it.

Adventures on a Solo Backpacking Trip
to Raspberry Lake

This year, as for the past two years, I decided to go on a backpacking trip into the wilderness for my birthday. My destination would be Raspberry Lake, a spot in the Siskiyou Wilderness Area I hadn't been to before. I only had time for an overnight stay, but two short days can host a lot of adventures, which I recount as follows:

The first thing that happened, before I even left the house, was that I lost a contact lens.

The next thing that happened was that in my rapt attention to *Listen and Learn Swedish* on the tape deck, I drove past the turn-off to the wilderness area and had to backtrack thirty miles.

The next thing that happened was that for seventeen steep, graveled miles, the car clattered like it had a rattlesnake seething in the trunk and mysteriously scraped bottom on places I thought gave ample clearance, so I should not have been surprised when I got to the trailhead to find my right rear tire chewed to shreds. It was noon. The heat was sweltering. I just wanted to put my pack on my back and head for the wilderness.

The next thing that happened was that for the first time in my life I changed a tire by myself.

Then I put my pack on my back and headed for the wilderness. I walked and walked, down into Youngs Valley and up the Elk Lick Trail, but I never saw where the trail forked to Raspberry Lake, as the map promised it would. The more I studied the map, the more confused I became. Was I on this trail or that one? Had I stopped here at a bend or there? Had I myopically missed the fork? Unable to determine my location, I hiked back a mile or so, walking close to this tree and that one to see if it held a trail sign and checking out every indentation in the woods that might be a trail. Finally I concluded that even if I were on the wrong trail, it was the only one, so wherever it went, there went I.

That trail got nicer and nicer, traveling high into views of the Devil's Punchbowl peaks and other rugged heights of the Siskiyous, then beginning to drop steeply, and the next thing that happened was that I began to wish I had thought to cut my toenails before I left home. Every down-hill step jammed my toes against my boots. Oh! How my toes hurt! Uphill was toil; downhill was pain. But I was dropping into a cirque at last, and soon I glimpsed the lake below me, dark green and wooded, and knew there would be an end to toenail torture. Gratefully and sufferingly, I minced my steps down to the lake.

The first thing I did was take off my boots. After a moment of utter relief I stripped down further and took a long swim, then made camp and ate dinner in view of a sunset that blazed gold, blinked, and went out. Even before the day was fully dark, I was stretched out in my sleeping bag, asleep.

The next thing that happened was that I woke up worrying about bears. Trying not to think about bears kept me awake for hours, but I finally fell asleep and woke up at 6:00 for a swim, and then the *next* thing that happened was that I took out the scissors on my Swiss Army knife and cut my toenails. After breakfast, I broke camp, took a last swim, and hit the trail, hiking into the worst heat of the day, but at least downhill was less pain, even if uphill was the same toil. And when I got to the car, at least I didn't have to change a tire.

The last thing that happened was that I ate a salad and an ice cream in town, then drove home and plopped into bed for a long night's exhausted sleep.

A Boy's Rite of Passage
in the Red Buttes Wilderness Area

The fourteen-year-old boy set out on foot with his father from Dutchman's Peak. The next day they met his mother, his sister, and some friends (I and nine others) in the Red Buttes Wilderness Area.

The next morning the celebrants gathered at a large, hollow pine tree with a hole for a doorway on one side and a round window on the other side which framed, from inside the tree, wildflowers, blue ridgelines, and the angel wings of Mt. Shasta. The friends sat in a circle behind the tree with the boy between his mother and his father, tied wrist to wrist to each with ropes of grass. He was presented with a quilt, each square of which was made by a different friend. He was given words of love and three tasks for his sojourn: to compose a poem about the quilt, to tell a story about a creature who lived in the Red Buttes, and to come back with something to make us laugh. He stood up, breaking the bonds with his parents. He stowed the quilt in his backpack, put the pack on his back, and walked out of camp towards Towhead Lake, where he would spend the next twenty-four hours alone in the wilderness.

The next morning the group built an arch of two stone columns with a curved, white log on top. They decorated it with flowers and pretty rocks and laid a line of tiny white rocks under it to form a threshold. Then the men left to meet the boy at the lake.

Several hours later, the women in camp, who had been devising their own contribution to the ritual, heard the men on the trail and quickly positioned themselves on the far side of the arch: one standing on a rock with a bent-stick "microphone," the other six, wearing improvised skirts and holding pine-needle pompoms, arranged cheerleader style. The initiate was blindfolded and carried to the arch, where the blindfold was removed. A little apprehensively he walked through the arch, at which moment the women broke into song with a Beach Boys' tune: "Our Jademan's back; it's a big celebration," pompoms shaking, skirts swishing, voices jubilant.

Joyfully, the initiate was encircled and led to the ceremonial tree, where the celebrants played "natural instruments" - resonant pieces of wood and seed-pod shakers. Under the soft rhythms we chanted our song: "Hey, hey, tell it well. You're part of the story I tell. Hey, hey, tell it well. We're a part of the story you tell." The initiate read his poem (which used the quilt as a metaphor for life), then crawled inside the tree while the celebrants trooped to the other side. Through the window of the tree he animated a chipmunk hand puppet who, clasping his little hands and bowing his head, told a story of his life at Towhead Lake that elicited delighted laughter. The three tasks had been accomplished.

Reassembled with the initiate behind the tree, the men and women gave him advice about life and presented gifts to him. He reentered the tree, into which, one by one, family and friends ducked, stooped, or crawled to congratulate him. Then all except the boy gathered on the far side of the tree, and he appeared in its window to announce himself to them using his new middle name. When he came out of the tree, each person filed past him, shaking his hand and greeting him by his full name. Finally, the ceremony at an end, the celebrants feasted and played games till the full moon shown waxy on the snowy wings of Mt. Shasta and illuminated the wildflowers of the meadow with blue luminescence.

The next day the stones of the arch were strewn into the dry creek bed, and the tired celebrants walked out of the wilderness to the trailhead. There the father and his son set their packs in the truck, got on their bicycles, and rode down the gravel road back to the valley and paved roads and finally back home.

The boy who had gone into the wilderness had returned a man.

Canoeing Klamath Lake

"We need the tonic of wildness," Thoreau said, "to wade sometimes in marshes where the bittern and the meadow-hen lurk...and to smell the whispering sedge where only some wilder and more solitary fowl builds her nest." Eight of us, for the tonic of wildness, slipped our canoes into the glass-smooth, lily-strewn, tannic-dark marsh of Klamath Lake. Immediately we were among the birds - the pied-bill grebe with its hurt-puppy whine, the resonating whistle of yellow-headed blackbirds, terns diving before, behind, and beside our canoes ("Never leave a tern unstoned," quipped Steve, expedition leader), harriers, cormorants, the great blue heron, a distant flock of sparkling pelicans, and America's great bald eagle. Quietly we paddled, listening to the birds, occasionally focusing binoculars on a distant bird.

Suddenly a subtle kerplunk changed the mood. My binoculars had slipped from my ten-year-old son's hand into the lake.

My heart sank with the binoculars. "You know those had belonged to my grandfather," I began, but Ela's misery silenced me. I put on my glasses and peered into the water.

The canoes had drifted, so we couldn't tell the exact spot where the binoculars had fallen in. Ela, in the stern, paddled; I leaned close to the water and watched. At first everything was murky and dark; then, three feet under the shadow of the canoe, the bottom emerged. "If we pass them, I'll see them," I said, heartened by the possibility but without much hope. Vegetation crowded the sandy bottom - waving arms of horsetail grasses, river lettuces, water ferns, marsh seaweeds. It was mysterious and beautiful, but I was worried about spoiling the canoe trip. Here we were watching the bottom of the lake instead of the birds, the clear-blue sky, the snowy peaks of Crater Lake that leapt abruptly beyond the flatness of the marsh, another world away. I sat up to say it wasn't worth it, but the sight of seven people leaning over their canoes to watch the bottom encouraged me - and I didn't really want to give up. I returned to my underwater exploration. Ela paddled slowly. "There they are!" I cried.

"Right there!" By this time we were already drifting beyond them, and I could no longer see them. Steve was there immediately, fishing with his paddle where I was pointing, and he brought up the binoculars.

We went on, gliding through the dark waters, past the bird-filled shores and hummocks, docking on a dike, and then, a little more quickly because lunch lay before us, paddling back towards camp. Ela, hungry, set a fast pace, but I wouldn't let him take the lead through this maze of waterways because although the way out seemed to be marked by "Hunter Access" signs, ambiguous turns between signs could easily confuse the route-seeker. "Let Steve stay in front," I cautioned my starving shipmate. "He's the guide." But there is no guide infallible; ours took a wrong turn, and the whole party was lost. Immediately hoots and jeers came from Steve's wife and two teen-age children, but, unperturbed and in a characteristically terse fashion, he answered, "I was watching the birds. We're too far south."

My arms were already dropping off, and the vision of paddling up and down various arms of the lake looking for the right water-path back to camp and lunch seemed more dismal than losing my binoculars. I had the impulse to tell Steve to find the right path and come back and tell us, but, of course, that was ridiculous. This was the time to practice my Taoistic philosophy. I turned around and continued listening to the birds, watching the monotonous and intimate landscape of the marsh, and paddling, paddling, mechanically paddling behind my guide. He retraced our canoe-steps one turn back, turned correctly, and we were almost home.

After lunch I waded into the marsh and dived into the shockingly cold, spring-fed water. A tern dived in front of me; a trout jumped to my left. A bald eagle circled the trees where she had her nest. Tall marsh irises dotted the shore; yellow monkey-flowers made small islands close to the spring. "It's the tonic of wildness," I thought, "and how we need the tonic of wildness!"

Messing About in Boats

"There is nothing - absolutely nothing - half so worth doing as simply messing about in boats. Simply messing - messing - about - in - boats; messing -" At this point in Rat's monologue to Mole in *The Wind in the Willows*, Rat's boat rams into the bank. I was as dreamy as Rat as I canoed down the upper Rogue River, but my boat stayed on course, due, I am sure, to my alert sternman, Badger. This was not the *Wind-in-the-Willows* Badger, who "simply hates society," but Rod Badger, gregarious and adept leader of this flotilla of eight canoes on a Sierra Club canoe trip. I was in the bow of Rod's graceful Au Sable, Ela in the bow of a big Grumman behind us, the rest of the group following.

The canoes floated gently downstream; paddling was effortless. A pinwheel of thistledown tumbled upriver; a dipper zipped in for an insect; a garden of ferns poised on a mossy log island. I dipped and swung my paddle, but the mosaic of underwater stones mesmerized me. I dipped again, and a hawk landing in a riverside fir riveted my eye from water to sky. As the canoe glided under morgue-gray, longitudinally ribbed, colossal pumice cliffs, I shivered; as we pulled into sunshine, I relaxed and smiled. Rich forest odors wafted to my nose; warm winds brushed my skin. "There is nothing - absolutely nothing - more worth doing...."

"Those big cliffs were made six thousand years ago by lava avalanches from the eruption of Mt. Mazama," Rod said from the stern. "Those gullies on the banks are beaver runs.... The man in the wooden canoe is writing a book about solo canoeing in Baja.... Stay centered" (in a canoe, he meant, but the application is life-wide), "and you can do anything." When I asked him why he had become a chemist, he said, "In college I was told I couldn't get a job as a wildlife biologist." (But what I had really wanted to know was why a man with such linguistic acuity had become a scientist.) "Look into those holes in the pumice cliffs," he continued, "and you'll see the charcoal remains of trees burned six thousand years ago."

How could I absorb the significance of that? The river carried me downstream, and I relapsed into Mole's attitude as he floated down river with Rat: "Absorbed in the new life he was entering upon, intoxicated with the sparkle, the ripple, the scents and the sounds and the sunlight, he trailed a paw in the water and dreamed long waking dreams."

It wasn't all pleasant dreaming - there were the portages. Four times we hauled seventy-to-ninety-pound canoes up slippery hills, over bulky logs, across treacherous beaver runs. I didn't mind. It was part of the wilderness canoeing experience, and, anyway, for the long portage Rod handed me our packs and paddles, heaved the canoe onto the support of his backpack, and took off through the forest. Lightly burdened, I followed easily behind him.

After lunch, Rod asked if I would like to take the stern. I was honored. I must have passed the bow test in spite of my dreams down the river; Rod would never trust the helm of his canoe to incompetence. But now I would have to stay alert. Ahead of us lay the only white-water thrill on this gentle-water trip: a small rapids bordered by Scilla and Charybdis, a rock shelf on one side and a jutting tree branch on the other. One by one the canoes made it through. Most of them, including mine, hit bottom as they shot out of the turmoil, but Ela razzed me because mine hit harder than his. Rod, however, had not criticized my navigation, and I was not unsatisfied. He told me, in fact, as we stepped ashore at the end of the journey, that I could take stern in his canoe any time. It was the supreme compliment.

I was reluctant to leave the water for the road. Rod agreed, quoting for me Rat's words from *The Wind in the Willows*. (Pretty good, I thought, for a chemist.) There was compensation, too, for leaving the river - huckleberry pie at Beckie's Cafe at Union Creek.

"If you're canoeing here," Rod said, "Beckie's huckleberry pie is *de rigueur*."

Pretty good vocabulary - for a chemist. And pretty good pie, too. Pretty good ending to a pretty good day.

The Idea of Summer

Our idea of summer is that it is the season of ease and pleasure, the time of year when the living is easy. But *New Yorker* writer Adam Gopnik scoffs at that idea. He says our concept of summer is but an American myth as big as our illusion of Christmas. The June 22 issue of the *New Yorker*, in which he made that comment, was called the summer fiction issue, which Gopnik seemed to interpret as the issue devoted to our fiction of summer.

"The American idea of summer," he writes, "is even more unreal than many of our other national devotions. The truth is," he says, "summer is white-and-brown skies, a muggy climate, an overworked population."

Oh, poor Adam Gopnik, so cynical he can't even see the summer in front of his face. The truth is that summer is lovely.

After all the rainy days and gloomy skies of last spring, we have been treated to weather so soft, gentle, and warm it wraps around the day like sleeping kittens. Birds whistle, sing, and warble from the edge of the woods all day long and are so beautifully noisy at dawn I lie in bed listening before getting up to go for a long walk in the woods. During the day I sit in my rocking chair in the shade of the cherry tree, surrounded by red roses and yellow day lilies, embroidering a wedding gift. The green carpet of the lawn tickles my bare feet; the warmth of the sun radiates from the other side of the shade. The sweet breath of honeysuckle, as sensuous as silk, drifts by. I push my needle in; I pull my needle out, painting pictures with thread. Does this sound like an overworked population?

When I tire of sewing, I pick up the book I am reading and spend another hour avoiding Adam Gopnik's American summer. I play my guitar on the porch, make fruit crepes for lunch, pick wildflowers. Finally, I say to myself, "Diana, you really must do some work," but the day is so peaceful I can't bear to disturb it with the hum of the generator, so instead of leaning over my computer to write my essay, I sit at my desk and pen a letter.

It's true I am shirking my duties. It's true such pandering to the sensual will have to stop. I can't dismiss every class session to give my students time to do their research (as I tell them). But does any of this sound like white-and-brown skies, a muggy climate, and an overworked population? Maybe the difference in summers is the difference between New York City and Applegate, Oregon, but I think Gopnik is on the right track. It's really a difference in ideas. My guess is that there are those in Oregon whose idea of summer is 100 degree weather, terrible mosquitoes, and bored kids hanging around the house all day. If summer is an idea, it's whatever idea we want to make it, and that's no different, really, Mr. Gopnik, from the rest of life.

Canning Peaches
as a Poetic Process

Right in the busiest time of my summer, I was given two forty-pound boxes of peaches. The peaches grew riper and riper, and still I couldn't find time to can. I desperately ate peaches morning, noon, and night; I gave peaches away; I made peach cobblers and peach cheesecake for potlucks and friends; I had peaches and yogurt every morning for breakfast; and yet, with increasing rapidity, more and more peaches were reaching the rotted stage. Finally, I found a few free hours and grabbed them for canning.

Canning cannot be hurried. A linear, logical, left-brain function, it calls for organization and step-by-step procedures. It reminds me of those exercises in paragraphing given to school children: "Put the following sentences in the proper order: Then she spread the bread with peanut-butter. Mary is making a peanut-butter sandwich. Finally she ate it. First she got the bread," and so forth. Straighten it all out, and you have the proper order of things, as in the canning process. To wit:

First I filled a canning pot with water and seven jars at the sink. Then I carried it, muscles bulging, across the room to the stove. I put on a smaller pot of water for blanching peaches, and I made a pan of honey syrup, but with the two big pots hogging the three-burner stove, the syrup had to wait on the counter, a sentence I hoped to fit into its proper place later. On the trunk opposite the stove I set, in the proper working order, a pan of cold water (to cool blanched peaches); a bucket for peels, pits and rotten peach pieces; a large bowl for peeled and pitted peaches ready for jars; and a knife.

Such linear preparation is prosaic, but there is poetry in the process of processing peaches. Six plump peaches plopped sensuously into the hot water. A minute later I slid them off my slotted spoon into the cold water and shipped six more in. And so it went. Quickly I began slipping peach-pink skins off golden, slippery peaches, halving the succulent insides, juice dripping through my fingers and down my wrists. Mosquitoes and buzz-flies zipped and buzzed around my head, but every swat splattered sticky peach juice, so with difficulty I restrained my temper. There could be no stopping. I ploughed through diminishing mounds of peaches till they all lay round and slimy, gleaming peachy-keen and ripe, ready for the bottling and the hot-water bath.

Into the jars I propped them, quickly, quickly, everything's ready; seal them up and into the bath. With a sigh the seven heavy jars sank into the water to rest there, bubbling, for thirty minutes. Meanwhile, I cleaned up. (That should always be the end of the Mary-makes-a-peanut-butter-sandwich exercise, but I've never seen it there.) When I brought the peaches up again, they were transformed, golden globes, glass jars of eclipsed suns, hemispheres of potential cobblers and winter breakfasts. I set them on top of the summer-unused wood stove, where, cooling and drying, one by one they popped their lids inward, proving their seals.

How admirable they looked! And all the peaches were finally accounted for, the boxes empty. There was not a peach in the house accessible to my gullet before Thanksgiving, before which it's sacrilege to break a seal. Not a peach in the house - so what would I have for breakfast?

Fire from the Dragon's Tongue

Like the many-forked tongue of a giant, celestial dragon, lightning ripped into the mountains. The tongue lashed out and the dragon roared, and the tongue lashed and the dragon roared, and finally the dragon roared and grumbled and grew more distant, but 1,659 strikes of its tongue had left their mark. Now the dragon, flying through the darkness of a sky flickered here and there with the fire of stars, could look down into the darkness below and see blazing stars flickering here and there in the mountains on fire.

As though the dragon is still breathing fire, the air is white with smoke. The sun rises a mass of flaming, boiling oils and, setting, flashes the burning reflection of fire into the eyes of southern Oregon the way a child playing with a mirror reflects the sun into a playmate's eyes. Daylight is an eerie orange-gold; shadows are gray-green. The smell of wet ashes or of burning wood occasionally drifts through the air, but generally the winds are mercifully still.

Some fires were perilously close. I could see one from my mailbox on the paved road, long loops of fire fringing the ridge tops at night like tinsel on a Christmas tree, thrilling, frightening, strangely beautiful if I could detach myself from what I was seeing, yet the strangest thing was to be there on the road watching - only watching - one of nature's most dangerous phenomena. One friend, having heard about the fires in southern Oregon on National Public Radio, called from Tennessee to make sure I was all right. He said I sounded remarkably calm, but what is there to do except watch and wait and be alert and then carry on with everyday activities? It's like waiting for the baby to arrive. You don't stop daily life because the baby is due; you go ahead with it, and you watch and wait and be alert, work in the garden, do the laundry, can the peaches, and when the time comes, you act.

In the meantime, with these forest fires threatening imminent danger, the days are tense with an underpinning of alertness, a sense of ominous foreboding stemming from the constant reminders that all is not well: the continual drone of bombers flying invisibly far overhead; the choppy roar of helicopters immediately overhead, dangling 500-gallon buckets of water; busloads of fresh firefighters passing up and down the road; clumps of weary ones lining the road at dark, waiting for buses and trucks to take them to food and rest, their yellow coats and their faces and helmets smeared with mud, dirt, and ashes; the ambulance turning up the old logging road now urgently marked "Fire"; the roar of bulldozers; the trucks and the water tankers and the CB radios and sometimes even the crackling voice audible over the CB: "Hey, Jack, better got out of there! It's going to go up in flames any minute!" - reminders that while I can peaches down here, up there men and women are swinging polaskis, manipulating bulldozers, directing water hoses, cutting through brush, logs, and trees to build fire lines and battle flames in an inferno of intense heat, choking smoke, scorching flames, trees crashing and stumps tumbling down the slopes like great balls of fire. The simple domesticity of canning peaches in the midst of this crisis makes me feel like Nero fiddling while Rome burns, but in actuality there is nothing to do except watch, wait, be alert, and go ahead and fiddle.

In this case Rome didn't burn. Like a rampaging bull finally corralled, the fire, though not controlled, has been contained. Its rage of damage and destruction has ended; it will die. And then what will we see in the wake of the fire? With wildlife, water, trees, steep mountainsides of forest communities affected, what will those dangerous dances of the dragon's tongue mean to both the ecology and the economy of southern Oregon? For years conservationists and timber companies have fought bitterly over the use of these forests. Will these burned-out acres create an even more bitter struggle over what is left? Or, during the scores of years it will take for the phoenix of these forests to rise out of these ashes, will we be able to see each other and our forests with different eyes in order to seek new solutions to old problems? The flickering dragon's tongue has sobered our outlook, not to make our struggles seem petty, but lest we forget that we are not the only players in the game.

A Close Call for Autumn

Southern Oregon lived under a false weather zone for so long during the fires of late summer I was afraid we would miss autumn altogether. I was afraid we would be sloughing along under our inversion-layer blanket of smoke, our eyes on the ground and our heads bent under our burden of oppression, while our golden autumn flew by unseen over our heads. I was afraid the trees, longing for sunshine, would turn brown, sag, and lose their leaves in a dispirited droop of giving up, and we would trudge into winter without ever greeting it with the banners of autumn.

But a few days ago I woke up to a sky clear and blue. Lovely snow-white clouds lifted and drifted high in a depth I had forgotten was there. At night stars sparkled in the zillions. The sky seemed to go on forever in its daytime blueness and nighttime blackness. My head lifted. I looked up and looked and looked, deeper and deeper; my step grew lighter, my eyes began to sparkle with the stars again, and my skin tingled with the warmth of a friendly sun.

The trees lifted their arms. Loren Eisley has said it is not only permissible but essential to anthropomorphize because if we don't anthropomorphize animals and rocks, we may eventually forget to anthropomorphize ourselves; so I will go on to say the trees looked up at that blue sky and grinned and burst into their normal autumn attire. Maples threw huge, sunny-gold, broad-fingered leaves at the sun; dogwoods fluttered into darkening reds, and viny maples deepened into wine-rich purple-reds at the edges of the forest. Alders laughed until they cried and tears of yellow dropped to their feet. Golden autumn had arrived at last.

The uplift of autumn has arrived, and the glory of autumn. The colors are here, and the crisp morning air and the cold nights warming gently into agreeably hot afternoons. The corn has dried brown on the stalk while pumpkins and winter squashes ripen orange and yellow. Flocks of south-tending birds resting on telephone wires silhouette against the blue sky. Ducks' wings make soft whirrings as flocks rise from the pond, circle, find direction, and fly steadily on.

There is a peremptory call in the autumn air, an urgency to prepare for the season to come - to see that the firewood is in, stacked neatly and fully in the back yard, a source of satisfaction and security; to insulate new hot water pipes; to seal the windows and skylights against the coming rain and cold. But it is more than that. The urgency in the air is for me to rise up and look around - to see and breathe, to remember that life is now, that while the sky is blue over my head and the leaves yellow, red, ochre, and orange, I must open my senses.

But yesterday when I opened my senses, I smelled smoke; when I looked up, I saw smoke pouring again over the mountain from the Red Buttes, crawling in from the Kalmiopsis, giving us ashy-brown horizons and hazy mountains again. For three glorious days I have ridden horseback, gone canoeing, and taken long walks. I have breathed deeply. For three days I have deified autumn. But, says Robert Frost,

> *Leaf subsides to leaf;*
> *So Eden sank to grief*
> *So dawn goes down to day.*
> *Nothing gold can stay.*

And, I suppose, it is ever true.

Cutting a Pattern from the Perfect Autumn

Season-makers, I think, should work from patterns. Variations from year to year would be allowed, but if the tailors would use patterns, they could cut the seasons according to what we already know is a perfect fit. My suggestion is that the tailors take this autumn as the pattern for all future autumns, since it is as near perfect as they come.

Consider, for instance, color. The tailors this autumn have eschewed the washed-out blandness of some years, pale, uninteresting fabrics, in favor of vividness and sharpness; they have shunned the monotony of last year's yellows in favor of a rich variety of hues and tints. We don't have to dig deep into our vocabularies to describe the trees; we can take one look and shout, "Red! Yellow! Bronze! Orange! Pink! Burgundy!" and then if we want to get closer, we can lean in and whisper, "Cinnabar. Magenta. Amber. Terra-cotta. Russet. Mauve. Ferruginous."

Next to color, the most important consideration for a perfect autumn is rain. A long autumn of dry days is wearing on the nerves, since we are never far from the thought that without winter water we face summer drought. Our spirits begin to dry up; we lose the spring in our step; we languish in gloom even under bright skies. On the other hand, an overly wet autumn doesn't give us a chance to breathe. When it rains too long, our spirits are dampened; our step becomes weighted; we peer at the sky as though from under water, looking for that blue that will give us a chance to come up for air. This autumn, which, as I say, should serve as the pattern, has given us a dash of rain now and then, every once in a while a good hard downpour to promise a strong, wet winter, and plenty of balmy, sunny days when we can breathe deeply and swim happily in autumn air.

Temperature is perhaps the most temperamental element of all, and tailors could maybe make some adjustments in this autumn along these lines. It's so easy to get things too cold or too warm and spoil the whole outfit. The very worst autumn weather is cold and dry, when it's so cold I have to leave the water running to keep it from freezing but so dry I'm afraid I'll drain the holding pond at the creek if I do. Too warm is just as bad; I don't want to feel like it's still summer after I'm teaching class again, and, besides, colored leaves go with cool weather like scones with tea, and cheese with wine. Autumn should be crisp, with nights cold enough to sweeten the apples and days just cool-tipped. This autumn has been a little too warm for the perfect pattern piece; we should have had a frost by now. The overall feeling isn't bad, day and night, but adjustments would be in order.

The night sky of autumn is important, too. It should be keen and lustrous, something with an edge to it, something tinged with excitement or desire. Imperfect autumn nights - too warm, too wet - seem a little warped, the stars globbed onto the sky with glue. Autumn nights that serve as the pattern have a crescent moon and a scattering of stars cut out by a precision die and incised into the sky.

So there you have it. That's how autumn ought to be, so let the pattern-makers take note: for color, rain, temperature, and night skies, this autumn is a perfect fit.

Autumn in Chiaroscuro Tints

What happened to the autumn color? Where are the golden yellows and the flaming oranges, the scarlets and the vermilions? Who dulled the brilliance? Who rubbed the blush from the complexions of the trees; who sucked the energy away; who gave us achromatism, pallor, wanness in our autumn this year?

Brown, brown, brown - everywhere, it's brown. On a road I drive frequently a long row of red cedars, interspersed tree by tree with broad-leaf maples, is usually an autumn checkerboard of green and yellow. This year the maples between the cedars are lifeless brown. Favorite trees here and there which started to turn colors have given in to brown. Yellow turned ocher, red turned russet, scarlet turned chestnut. Far from being vibrant and exciting, the woods have become dull: spiritless, wearisome, prosaic, lackluster, humdrum, drab, and monotonous. The woods this year are brown.

Is this lack of color a depiction of weather past? Or a prediction of weather to come? Does it mean we had a hot summer? A dry year? A late fall? Or does it mean it will be an early winter? A dry winter? A hard winter? It must mean something; what kind of energy is sucking at the roots of the trees, drawing their color right out of their skins?

Things are bad if I had rather look at my calendar picture than at the mountains themselves. How can I accept brown? Well, first I should stop pining for gold. Once I stopped looking for Renoir, I found Rembrandt. In a reversal of art history, we have gone from large areas of pulsating color to a soft, retreating chiaroscuro. Brown is not just brown; if it were, the *Mona Lisa* and *The Night Watch* would be dull pictures, prosaic, lackluster, humdrum, and monotonous.

Brown is a vast spectrum of variations. Brown in one tree is sudan brown, in another arabian brown, in another vassar tan, a real term for a real color, a term derived, in reality, from Vassar College, but my dictionary doesn't say whether it originated from the color of the New England trees around Vassar College or from the tan the

41

girls returned to school with after their Christmas vacations in Florida. Some trees are chestnut brown, some pearl-brown, some sand brown. Some are somber umber; others burnt sienna, sienna brown, or sienna drab. Are the trees this autumn sienna drab? It's a real color, a "light grayish brown to reddish brown that is duller than sandstone and paler than wood rose." Sandstone? Wood rose? What beautiful colors! Some trees seep with sepia: "a dark grayish yellowish brown that is stronger and slightly yellower than seal and stronger and slightly yellower and lighter than otter." Seal and otter, too? Other trees are only ocher, "a moderate orange that is yellower and deeper than honeydew, yellower and darker than Persian orange, and duller than mikado orange." Honeydew? Persian orange? Mikado orange? All that in the autumn woods? Wood rose, seal, otter, honeydew, mikado? How could I ever have thought this a dull autumn?

A Rhapsody on Yellow

Never was there such a yellow as has been given us this fall. Black oaks and broad-leaf maples are deeper and more vivid with yellow than ever before. Willows, hazels, and alders are yellow as usual, but viny maples, dogwoods, and poison oak are not their usual scarlet red, russet red, and ruddy pink, but are yellow instead. One grove of viny maples droops in a creamy, pale yellow canopy; another grove tried to turn to red - I counted five scarlet leaves - but yellow predominated, sometimes streaked or edged with red, like flames that blacken and curl paper, but yellow, nonetheless. Poison oak, it seems, would be red or nothing, but red isn't available this year, so poison oak branches stand stark naked while oaks and maples and dogwoods all around it swirl in cloaks, capes, and coats of yellow. Dogwoods, usually peachy pink, are this year peachy yellow. Are viny maples and dogwoods botanical chameleons that they respond in color to some atmospheric conditions invisible, inaudible, and indefinable to me? Willows, hazels, bracken ferns, alders, too, are all yellow, some paler, some brighter, but all yellow. A walk through the woods this autumn is a walk through yellow.

Vibrant and exuberant, these trees leap through the evergreen forests like tongues of fire. This autumn we have been given majesties of yellow, ecstasies of yellow, deep lakes of yellow pressed against the sky. "If only I could simply let go with my feet," I think, looking up into a sky of maple yellow, "I could float in that yellow like swimming through the blue of the lakes." Yogically it should be possible. I should be able to just lift...just let go...just become one with yellow as with blue.... Yogically and theoretically it must be possible, but my feet stay firmly planted on the ground, rooted there by gravity, and yellow eludes me in those lofty clouds of leafy yellow. Only the trees - only the special trees given the privilege - know yellow in such exuberance it soars above the earth and shouts towards heaven like the brassy ring of trumpets and cymbals.

Giving Plants and Animals Their Due

When Salmon Go Up the River
and Geese Fly South

The salmon are running. They are thrashing upstream, bucking the current, jumping the rapids to reach at last their birthing place which would now be their dying place. The salmon are running on the Rogue River, and with a years-long burning to see the famed fish, I, too, am on the Rogue, paddling a canoe downstream against the upstream-struggling salmon. Splotched grey, black, and white, the old, battered bodies are already decaying. They look like sharks as their fins break the top of the water, and they thrash and spin in small groups in the river as they fight their way upstream. Had I expected a sense of brilliant purpose here, of heroic gallantry, of last-gasp effort in the necessity to spawn before dying? Should I be looking for the live representation of the end in the beginning and the beginning in the end?

An unmistakable honk in the sky snaps my head upward to see a long V of geese, flying with a satisfying sense of direction and purpose on their long trek south. It's a no-nonsense sort of feeling, a get-down-to-business-and-stay-there attitude, the V itself the pointed symbol of azimuthal direction even as the salmon are the alpha and omega, the primal drive for completion. Perhaps I, too, should strive for such directiveness. Do those who live lives of salmon-spawning and wild-goose sense of purpose live lives of heroics and achievements?

Those are images of the businesslike - the upright, sensible, direct, logical, hard-edged, unfanciful, and forceful. Those are images for the practical people. Robinson Jeffers says that practical people

> Weary of the sea for his waves go up and down
> Endlessly to no visible purpose;
> Tire of the tides, for the tides are tireless, the tides
> Are well content with their own march-tune
> And nothing accomplished is no matter to them.
> It seems wasteful to practical people

*Im*practical people would perhaps prefer the image of other flocks of migrating birds, flocks in which the image is pattern, rhythm, and movement: aesthetics, not purpose. The undulating group patterns of one flock break and collect and break again in visual diminuendos and crescendos. Suddenly sucked into the top of a tree, the birds disappear; spewed forth later, they are belched out as on the blows of a bellows. Another flock flies low against the hills, the slant of the morning sun striking from them a flutter and sparkle like a thousand maple leaves skittered horizontal by an autumn wind. The irregular undulations of another flock wave black across the sky from one end to the other - fans opening and closing in a coquettish hand, an accordion waving and weaving its music, leaves in the wind, waves and ocean swells and music swells and the opening and closing of a body of dancers at a ballet.

But inspiration in geometry, Pushkin said, is just as necessary as in poetry. Yin and yang are one symbol; birds and fish make one Escher metamorphosis. Migrating birds do finally make it south no matter how much energy they waste fluttering randomly, flying in curves and curlicues, and the beauty of the geese flying in their V against a dawn-rose sky makes as aesthetic an image as motley salmon swirling up the river.

The World Is Not a Zoo

Seeing wildlife is one of the exciting things about being in the wilderness. You come home, and friends say, "Did you see any bears?" and you say, "Yes, I saw a bear catching fish in the river and a fawn in a thicket and an osprey's nest with three babies in it; a pair of pileated woodpeckers and a king snake and a squirrel and a million mosquitoes," and you check your list to make sure you mentioned everything.

And so we see the world of nature as some wild and enormous zoo established and run for our benefit and pleasure, a wildlife safari park through which we travel hoping to see the exotic creatures poised there specifically for us to add to our lists. Yes, I've seen, in the wild, bears and eagles and elk; I've seen a moose and mountain sheep and an otter and a mink. And yesterday I saw one broken half of a tiny, thin fragilely blue robin's egg, and with that empty half-shell, the zoo ceased to exist. I was peeking inside the world of creatures who live their lives birthing, eating, procreating, and dying in a world a part of and yet apart from my own.

What story had poured out of that empty eggshell? Had some unimaginably tiny baby bird cracked the shell open to tumble into this large cosmic egg of unforeseeable complexities and multidimensions? Had that ugly little naked bird shaken its shell loose from its back, peeped and shrieked and cried till a big fat juicy worm was poked down its throat? Or had some snake - some skunk or porcupine - found the nest and the tiny eggs, broken them open, and supped on dainty raw robin's eggs? I held the miniscule, jagged-edged eggshell in the palm of my hand, its weightlessness indicating false insignificance, for with it I touched a world of mysteries and wonder.

A little brown bunny on the path to my house didn't hop away till I was quite close, and I said, "Watch out, little brown bunny, for the big white cat," and the next day there was little brown bunny fur by the big white cat's dinner dish. Today, again, a little bush rabbit was in the road, and again it didn't hop away till I had come quite close. Why do these rabbits stay so dangerously vulnerable? Why are there so many rabbits this summer when I seldom saw them before? And what wild creature bites my water pipe and why? Is it a coyote who bites the pipe to drink the water that squirts out? No, my neighbor and woods-teacher says, it's a bear, and he bites the pipe because he hears the water going through and thinks it's bees. But how do we know why he bites the pipe? We may know that it's a bear and not a coyote by other signs, but how will we ever know what the bear thinks when he bites a hole in the water line?

When you throw a flat stone a certain way, it will skim across the top of the water in a series of hops. Rocks skip, but why rocks skip science doesn't know. Presumably science could find out, but so far, I understand, no one has been motivated to explore the question, so skipping rocks remain a mystery. That's very nice. We need mystery in the universe. The universe is bigger than we in all ways, and we don't live here alone. The world, after all, is not our zoo.

My Contract with the Spiders

My contract with my spiders says I won't kill them and they will build their webs only in out-of-the-way spots. Once a week I am allowed to destroy webs with the stick end of a used piece of incense, so if the spiders want to chance weekly apocalypse, their part of the contract says they can build their nests.

Once a year, in the spring, I have the right to wipe the entire house clean of spider webs. I do not have to acknowledge that the tiny white dots nestled in a web are eggs. I can stab my incense stub into every sticky web and twist it round and round till the entire web balls itself into a cotton-candy glob that's as hard to scrape off the stick into the dustpan as to pull chewing gum off a shoe. Evicted spiders can rebuild if they can find a place, but in this season of spider-web demolition, places safe from the inescapable advance of the cleaning urge are hard to find.

Thus I have lived companionably with my house spiders, I untroubled by squeamishness, they free from worry of death by duster.

This winter I read an essay by Gordon Grice called "The Black Widow." Among other things, I learned that the bite of the black widow can cause sweats, vomiting, swelling, convulsions, and dozens of other symptoms and is so painful the doctor often asks, as a diagnostic question, "Is this the worst pain you've ever experienced?"

Squeamishness consequently accompanied my entire spring house-cleaning. Every spider web twirled into a ball by my incense stick attracted, like flypaper, images of the worst pains I have known - childbirth, rectal abscess, second-degree burns - and I quailed to think that none of those could have registered as high on the thermometer of pain as the bite of the black widow spider I hoped to goodness wasn't watching me now.

A black widow's web, Grice says, is "a messy-looking tangle in the corners and bends of things." But all the webs I found seemed like tangled messes in the corners and bends of things, so I turned for identification to Grice's tale of his mother vengefully running her stick through the dirty silver web of a black widow. "As it tore," Grice says, "it sounded like the crackling of paper in fire," a sound he claims is unique to the black widow's web.

As I washed up and down the house, running my stick through dirty silver webs, I listened for this crackle, and, yes! that was it! And there, in the next spider web! Isn't that what paper sounds like when it burns? Or is it? I twisted webs into cotton-candy balls, listening carefully, but finally decided I didn't know the sound of paper crackling in fire. So I threw some paper onto the fire and listened. With a soft whoosh! the paper burst into flames; silently it burned; with a faint tch-tch-tch-tch it settled into ash. Is that what Grice meant by a crackle? I tore the next spider web; it sounded exactly like the paper I had just burned.

In spite of Grice I still honor my contract with the spiders. I don't kill them, and they allow me to keep my house free of visible cobwebs. Lurking in the uneasy part of my brain, however, as I tear tangled messes of spider webs from the corners and bends of things, is the haunting phrase, "It's the worst pain you've ever experienced."

The Scourge of Scorpions

It was all very well for Cinderella to befriend the mice, but what would she have done with my scorpions?

Every year I find four or five scorpions in my house. Once I took my nightgown off its nail on the closet wall, and just before I slipped it over my head, a scorpion fell out. Once one fell on the stove as I was cooking dinner for a guest from France. Last spring when I was doing some house repairs, I tore out the built-in couch under my front windows and found six scorpions, not all at once in a clump, but six, one at a time. I put each in a jar and took it far into the woods.

In *The Beauty of the Beastly,* Natalie Angier tells us that some scorpion species are cannibals. I was hoping my scorpions were of that sort, but if that were true, I probably wouldn't have found six in one relatively small space. On the other hand, I am fervently hoping my scorpions are not of the "handful of giant species," Angier says, "that live cooperatively in harmonious colonies." I don't think mine are of the giant kind, but, not too long ago, when I heard the characteristic scritch-scritch-scritch of a scorpion in the black plastic that covers my ceiling insulation, I curiously scratched my fingernail in that spot, and the skittering took off in two, maybe three, directions. It sounded like a colony to me, but I prefer to think these scorpions were having a cannibalistic feast.

Angier has more facts to make me nervous. Scorpions can live for up to a year without eating, she says, so I guess a tactic of starving them out of the house wouldn't work. It is a lousy tactic, anyway, because there are plenty of insects and spiders in my house for them to eat. In fact, should I be glad there are scorpions here because they keep the spider population down? Maybe the number of scorpions diminishes the number of wasps. Anyway, scorpions aren't at the top of the food chain. Maybe I should bring in bats and snakes to eat my scorpions.

I also learned that scorpions can live from fifteen to twenty-five years - "and perhaps beyond," says Angier. Since I built this house about twenty-five years ago, some of us may have been living together that long. One should be careful with such loyal housemates.

Scorpions have been around in the same form for 400 million years. Like Minerva, they popped into the world fully developed. That should make newcomers like homo sapiens respect the beast. They also, Angier says, shine in the dark. The exoskeleton of the scorpion, she informs us, is made of chitin, which "reflects the ultraviolet rays from moonlight and other light sources so brightly that even a black scorpion will be a fluorescent shade of green or pink." But this is fascinating! Why is it that on these brilliant full-moon nights I don't see pink and green scorpions dancing in the rafters of my house? I know they're there. And how I would like to see the show! Once, anyway. Once would be enough. After that I think I would rather not know how many scorpions dance glowingly in the night over my head.

I never kill a scorpion if I can help it. I try to keep my scorpion karma clean because scorpions, I have come to believe, are highly psychic creatures. It's not Angier who leads me to this belief; she doesn't mention this fact. It is because every time I dream about a scorpion, I awake suddenly, fully aware. I lie still, terrified, desperately trying to blot out visions of the scorpion dropping on the baby's cradle in *The Pearl*; then I leap out of bed. I turn on the flashlight and begin the search. Every single time I have dreamed about a scorpion I have found a scorpion. And if that isn't enough to convince you, listen to this story. Some friends were visiting me from Tennessee: husband, wife, and teen-age son, Zach. Zach, who slept on the living room floor, got up one morning and said, "I dreamed about a scorpion last night. I've never dreamed about a scorpion before." Uh-oh, I thought, but I didn't say anything. Sure enough, later that morning I found a scorpion on the floor.

And with such creatures, wouldn't you want to keep your karma clean, too?

A Plague of Skunks

I came home from a three-week vacation in December to find that the storm-winds had not blown the roof off the house, the crush of snow had not broken my skylights, nor had rain poured through unexpected leaks in the roof. But the minute I set foot inside the house I knew what calamity had struck - skunk! That night my eyes validated what my nose had found. A little civet cat, the mountain skunk, poked his head under the closet curtain, looked at me (wondering why I was there), and helped himself to the cat's food. All night I could hear him stomping across the floor as though on hard plastic snowshoes, crashing through the jars in the pantry, skittering through the walls of the house. I tossed and turned and cursed the skunk roundly; the next morning, bleary-eyed, angry, and determined, I called the county trapper. He would be here the next day.

"Skunk," I chortled, "your days are numbered."

When Dean Lowe arrived at my house, he sniffed the air expertly. "Civet cat," he diagnosed. "Worse than the one-striped skunk of the valley." I was pleased; anything this bad ought to take honors for being the worst. Dean set his Hav-a Hart trap in the civet cat's path and baited it with cat food. "But there might be two," he warned. "This is mating season."

After he left, I went to town and didn't return until dark. To my joy, my flashlight revealed a civet cat scratching around inside the cage. Well, I thought triumphantly, there he can stay till Dean comes to cart him away. And I was feeling happy, smug, and relieved until I went inside and sat down to dinner and who should come scratching around the firewood and poking his nose in but Skunk #2? I was dismayed, but I had been prepared, so, okay, I could put up with one more night of hearing a skunk clatter through the pantry.

Dean came up the next day carrying an old tarp. Slowly, very, very slowly, he crept up to the cage and covered it, and then, fearless but careful, he carried it down the hill to his truck.

Good-by and good riddance, dear skunk.

Dean returned shortly with the cage and set it up in the same spot. I worried that the second skunk might have learned from the experience of the first and not be so easy to catch. "You're humanizing," Dean chastised. "Don't humanize."

He must have been right because that night, well after dark, I heard a very satisfying metallic "chink" as the trap door closed and then a scrabbling at the wire as the skunk realized he (or she) was caught. If I had felt smug, triumphant, happy, and relieved with the first skunk, I was ten times so with its mate. My troubles, I thought, are over.

So what was this pattering I could hear as of someone wearing big plastic snowshoes? What was this rattling around the cat's dish as of someone snitching a pellet?

I turned on the flashlight and waited, and in a minute or two a little striped fellow with a long pointed nose pranced cautiously into view. Dismay doubled. Then the civet cat screams began. Eeeee! Eeeee! This one in the house, running through the walls, screaming and squealing, the one outside, now screaming, now scratching at the cage. Eeeee! Eeeee! So why did I think I could hear a scrambling in my indoor woodpile again? Sounded just like a skunk - but one skunk was trapped and gone, that skunk was in the cage, and that skunk was in the wall - and then this skunk poked his inquisitive, brazen little nose under the curtain. Four skunks?! Skunks galore! I was in a horrifying fairy tale; some evil demon had put a spell on my house. Kill one skunk, and another appears. Catch that one, and two take its place. I was afraid to catch those two. Four more? Eight more? Civet cats forever? What did the sorcerer's apprentice do about his brooms? Must I resort to witch's brews and magic incantations, to esoteric spells for expelling skunks?

No, I need not. Dean Lowe, woods wizard, could come and work his magic on my skunks. Perhaps, not being as enamored of fairy tales as I, he wouldn't be caught in them; not seeing me as bewitched and under an evil spell, he could with patience, persistence, and nitty-gritty practicality, rid my house of its plague of skunks.

Opossum Wisdom

One night, hours after I had gone to bed, I was awakened by something big knocking around my fruit bowl in the kitchen area under my bedroom loft. Stealthily I leaned to the end of the loft and opened the flashlight into the room below, catching in its beam an opossum.

"Hey! Get out of there! Get!"

Startled, he took a few steps and stopped. Down from the loft flew books: *Corelli's Mandolin*, *The Harem Within*, *Possession*. The 'possum did a little two-step and froze. As *Cold Mountain* went hurtling off the loft, I remembered about 'possums. They don't run. They play dead.

I climbed down the ladder, grabbed the ashes shovel, and whacked the dead 'possum on the rump, at which he jumped into life and, urged on by the little iron shovel, waddled quickly out the door and onto the deck. He ran right over its edge and hit the deck below, then trundled off to nurse his bruises, while I climbed back into bed to ponder the puzzles of the 'possum.

Defense in nature comes in three forms - flight, fright, or fight, and in each form, humans have borrowed wisdom. Like rattlesnakes, we are quick to fight in defense. Like gila monsters, we know the psychological advantage of self-confidence and bravado. When chased by bees, we react like deer, and when white-water rafting we use a variation of this flight defense, facing danger and backing away from it.

But the natural world has a very strange fourth defense mechanism. "Danger!" says the ostrich, sticking her head in the sand, says the 'possum, playing dead. "I'm not here if I think I'm not."

In spite of having asked for centuries whether a falling tree makes a sound if no one hears it, humans reject the opossum's sense of reality. We know that in all kinds of situations - physical danger, emotional turmoil, domestic strife - the 'possum response won't work. While we are doing nothing, trouble gets worse. While our heads are in the sand, our enemies strike. While we're pretending they don't see us, they laugh at us and do us in.

So why hasn't the opossum been done in?

The evolution of the opossum has meant its survival, so maybe we can learn something from this strange marsupial. But we should not apply 'possum wisdom if confronted by a cougar, since a still prey excites a cat's curiosity, nor if facing an angry rattlesnake, in which case the white-water-rapids plan is best, nor if opposed by an angry spouse, who, feline-like, might paw at us until we react.

Nonetheless, we do find 'possum wisdom among philosophers and poets. Emerson, Longfellow, and Disraeli, among others, have told us that "all things come to those who wait." Lao Tzu said, "Do nothing, and all things will be done," and maybe even the Bible suggests something of the secret the opossum knows: "Be still and know that I am God." We may not understand how the opossum has survived with such a dumb defense, but maybe if we would just be still, we might found out the 'possum's wisdom, too.

Birds' Eggs and Birds' Song

I wouldn't even have noticed the little wren I found one day on a walk through the woods, except that he was so loud. Clowning on a viny maple limb over a thicket of salal, blackberry brambles, and honeysuckle vines, hopping and twittering and winking, chattering insistently, he wanted my attention, and so, of course, being a perverse human being, I did just what he was trying to keep me from doing: I looked around for a nest. I soon saw his tiny mate, twitching nervously on a limb just above the tangled undergrowth on the other side of a decaying log. Next I should peer over the log, move into the thicket, and search for the nest. How very special it would be - I imagined the catch of my breath - to see the wrens' nest, maybe even their tiny eggs. The biologist Bernd Heinrich described his childhood obsession of collecting birds' eggs as "a pleasure so great it didn't seem that it could be morally right." He found his first four tiny eggs when he was eight years old. Cradled on feathers in a nest of moss, lichens, and spiderwebs, greenish blue with purple and lavender splotches and black squiggles, they were, he said, more beautiful than anything he had ever seen. "I knew I had found paradise," he said. Would I be able now to witness that same secret paradise?

My foot hesitated on the brink of the log. These wrens were my neighbors. How could I go nosing around their home, trampling over their yard, trying to catch a glimpse of their bedroom? For what? It didn't seem to be morally right. I backed away quietly and left the wrens to return to their paradise unhampered and unobserved.

Some naturalist I'd make.

I envy Heinrich his knowledge of the beauty of birds' eggs. But in my clumsy, untutored way I can't stumble through the birds' thickets in search of that hidden beauty. For me, it will have to stay hidden. I'll have to find that beauty in the sunset-bright flash of an oriole at the edge of a field or the sudden fall of the scent of wisteria in my yard, in the arrangement of pale to deep pink phlox under the firs on my path or the dark shadow of a trout under the waterfall in the forest behind my house. It is not in the seeking or in the rarity but in the recognition that lies that which is more beautiful than anything else we have seen.

Besides, the birds have other gifts more freely given than the beauty of their eggs. Walking with a friend recently who could identify birds by their songs, I was impressed not only that he could name birds without seeing them but that he could hear them so well. I had been walking along thinking about this and that; he emptied his mind of its internal chatter, stopped, cocked his head, and let the sounds enter. I'm not listening when I'm talking, silently or out loud, and if I'm not listening I can't hear.

The growth of the musician, my guitar teacher says, is a progression in the ability to hear. Is it any exaggeration, then, to say the birds, who teach me to hear, have become my guitar teachers? And for that gift, in gratitude, I leave with them the secret of the beauty of their eggs.

Thirteen Ways of Seeing an Owl

1. To the Cherokee Indian, mythological brother. Before the beginning of Time, Thunder sent Lightning to a tree on an island to create fire. When the raven tried to retrieve the fire, it scorched his wings black. When the screech owl tried, a blast of hot air burned his eyes, turning them red. When the hoot owl and horned owl tried, the fire blew ashes into their eyes, making white rings. These birds carry the mark of the fire even today.

2. To the Middle Ages, wisdom. Thus Merlin, the wise magician at King Arthur's court, carried an owl on his shoulder.

3. In France, omen to a pregnant woman. If she hears an owl, she knows she will have a girl.

4. In Wales, an omen to an unmarried woman. If she hears an owl, she knows she will lose her virginity soon.

5. In Greece, the mascot of Athens. In ancient Greece, during a battle between Athenians and Persians, all the little owls (*Athene noctura*) that nested in the cliffs near the Acropolis gathered into a large flock and descended onto the Persian soldiers, confusing and frightening them so that the Athenians won the battle. (Note the connection with the Medieval concept of the owl as a symbol of wisdom, since Athena, the patron goddess of Athens, is the goddess of wisdom.)

6. In China, a snatcher of souls. "Did you hear the owl? He's digging the grave."

7. To Shakespeare, too, an omen of death. "It was the owl that shrieked, the fatal bellman,/Which gives the stern'st good-night," Macbeth said, all jumpy because he had heard an owl on this, the night he was supposed to kill the king.

8. To Job, an associate of the afflicted: "I am a brother to dragons," said Job, "and a companion to owls."

9. To the logger, threatened economic stability. "Eat an owl; save a logger."

10. To the environmentalist, an indication of forest health. "If you kill the owls, you kill the forest."

11. To me as a child, mystery and fear. The eerie scream of a screech owl sent shivers down my back as I sat reading in the Big Chair late at night, when the rest of the household had long ago gone to bed and the woods became bigger and deeper and the shriek of an owl was the wail of a child or the cry of the murdered.

12. To me after my automobile accident last fall, totem. Driving alone through the dark, silent forest towards home at midnight after a play in Ashland, I fell asleep at the wheel. The car, on an uphill slope, slowed, veered right, scraped against a tree, spun a complete circle, and slammed into the ditch on the opposite side of the road. Awaking terrified in a massive cloud of dust that was heavy with the smell of hot metal, I crawled out the window on the uphill side and assessed the damage. Both legs worked, my head was in one piece, and there was no blood. Damage to the car could be assessed later; I was only two miles from home, and so I started walking, striding up the road with long, strong steps, uttering cougar-protection spells that probably weren't necessary, anyway. With all the adrenaline, I could have fought off any mountain lion.

When I strode into the house, I was startled to find an owl sitting on my writing desk. Unlike most birds that get trapped in the house, this one was not panicked and did not fly from me when I approached but only stared at me out of its wide, wise, yellow eye. I opened the window over the desk and touched the owl gently on the back of the head, suggesting immediate flight before the cats returned. The owl lifted its wings and flew through the window, over the honeysuckle and into the night.

I now carry the totem of an owl - the one who stays awake at night - in my car at all times.

13. To the owl: The owl sits and looks, listens, flies, eats, sleeps, mates, and calls. The owl is.

Coming to Terms with the Deer

"Diana, you must have a garden," declared my friend, noting the delight I took in the bouquet she had brought me from her garden and the deer-thwarted efforts of my own yard. "You're a gardener; you had a garden once; you love flowers. Why don't you put a fence around your whole place to keep the deer out?" She suggested I put it deep in the woods where I wouldn't see it, and she admitted it would be expensive, "but," she said, "think of all the money you've already spent feeding the deer."

Now, that was true.

So I thought about it. I envisioned my house and garden enclosed by the unseen fence. But in that vision no opossums or porcupines ever wandered past my house any more, nor did I ever hear the nocturnal cooing warble of a raccoon calling to her babies from below my garden. I never again saw a cougar prowl through my back yard ; I never startled another bear in the woods behind the house, and there was no chance, now, of ever seeing a fox here or a coyote. Birds still sang from the treetops at dawn, and bats caught insects at dusk, but I never again disturbed a young buck napping on the bare ground of the path to my house and watched him rise casually at my approach and amble off. I never again saw, as I did yesterday, two does tiptoe past my house followed by two tiny, white-dappled fawns. I had put up "No trespassing" signs for the wildlife. I had made a demarcation between me and them. I had cut myself off from my surroundings to live in my own, different, separate world, as inappropriate as an island paradise in a desert.

I didn't like that vision, so I concentrated on the accompanying vision of the paradise, my little cottage surrounded by its English flower garden. It was quite beautiful; I was growing bountiful flowers and luscious vegetables - but it was all possible only by the fence. And I didn't want the fence. I wanted to live with the wilds as I always had, and luscious English gardens don't grow in the wilds. The two concepts are incompatible.

And so I have come to terms with the deer at last. The deer may stay. They may wander through my yard and eat what they want, and I might get exasperated, and I might yell at them from time to time, but the deer are as welcome here as the hummingbirds in the honeysuckle, the moonlight on the lawn, and the bears in the woods. I'll keep the deer out of my petunias with individual chicken-wire fences. I'll plant more of the flowers I have that I already know they won't eat: peonies, Shasta daisies, red-hot pokers, foxgloves. I'll trellis my wisteria, honeysuckle, and climbing rose out of their reach; I'll put planter boxes on my decks and fill them with lettuces, tomatoes, and drooping swoops of trailing lobelia. I'll probably still be lured into buying pretty flowers at the nursery only to find I've spent the money just to feed the deer, but I'll think about the cost of a fence, and I won't mind.

When I see the Western tanager flashing yellow and red in the cherry tree as it gorges on my fruit, I don't begrudge him that food. I share the foxgloves with the bees and the daisies with the butterflies. I'll share a little of my flowers with the deer, too, and maybe we can all live here in the wilds in peace together from now on. It is our paradise, not my island. Welcome, all.

My Nemesis, the Dog

When I returned home from the swimming hole to find garbage strewn here and there about my yard, I was irritated. When I found my compost dug up and stinking, I was annoyed; but when I returned home from an hour of tennis with Ela, both of us drooling in anticipation of the rhubarb pie still cooling in the kitchen, only to find the rhubarb pie smashed into the rug, the pie dish broken, and the pie half eaten, I was furious. The back of my camel of patience broke. Hatred seethed.

She's not my dog. I don't even want a dog, and if I did, it wouldn't be this one. She has desecrated my house, defecated on my lawn, and dedicated herself to my misery, for she won't leave. Desperately I tell her how much I hate her, get out of here, and all the ugly invectives I have on my tongue-tip. She turns sideways to me, sinks on her haunches, and squints her eyes, masochistically lifting her head the better to hear the abuse. Uriah Heapishly she cowers and cringes. Sickened, I turn away, but when I come out the front door again, she is still lurking in the yard. I pick up a rock to throw at her, a piece of pumice about as heavy as Ela's nerf ball, even before this dog chewed it to bits and scattered the pieces about the yard. I toss it at her. It bounces off her stomach, and she turns onto her back for more.

"Get out of my yard!" I yell. I implore; I beg. She squints and grins and winces her eyes, thumping her tail encouragingly. I try kicking her, but my kick is the mere suggestion of a shove, and the dog lies like a bag of sand, a cancerous tumor on the breast of my lawn. Her tail thumps the grass.

Ela told me her former owner used to beat her. Oh, God. Sympathy, now, as well as hatred? Unadulterated hatred is so simple; tangled with sympathy it becomes too complicated. I can't stand this weasling, sneasling, wimpy dog, yet I can't stand hating her, either. Is it her fault she's such a pitiful specimen of doghood, poor, despicable creature? You can't hate what you have such pity for. Would she in response to love and caresses metamorphose into a beautiful butterfly of a dog? Maybe, but I don't want to provide her that cocoon because in the meantime I would still have the worm.

Parasitically, she sticks to me like a tick to a dog. I want her no more than the dog wants the tick. But there is a solution. I can get rid of the parasite. If the dog won't leave and the owner won't keep her, I can take her to the Humane Society. That problem is easily enough solved. The other problem, not the dog but the emotional response to the dog, looms larger. If pity can subdue hatred, as I have seen that it can, then can I also learn to love beyond that pity?

Applegate Alders

Gerard Manley Hopkins, a nineteenth-century English poet, loved the beauties of the natural world. He was especially fond of a particular grove of aspens, which, he said, "quelled, and quenched in leaves the leaping sun." For me, my grove of alders on Highway 238 grabbed the sun and trunk-hugged it tight till, squeezed and teased, absorbed with the force of the alders, it burst out of the grove with a reddish-gold glow. Hopkins' aspens "dandled a sandalled shadow that swam or sank on meadow and river and wind-wandering weed-winding bank," but I knew of my alders nothing more than that sometime, infrequent radiance.

In 1879 Hopkins' "Binsley poplars," his aspens, were cut down. "All felled, felled, are all felled!" he cried, and I echoed him on the day of devastating discovery when I drove past my grove of alders and - gone! Stumps were left and a few remaining trees, the thinness of which would never capture the sun's light as the thick bulge of trunks had in the past. Surely the fellers of these alders di not know what they were doing. "O if we but knew what we do," lamented Hopkins, "when we delve or hew - hack and rack the growing green."

"It had better be a whale of a gorgeous house," I growled as I watched the clearing of that bit of land by the highway, afraid all the while it would be a mobile home.

But I was wrong on both counts. My alders were cut not for a home but for three or four head of cattle. These cattle are *not* as beautiful as my grove of alders. They do *not* give me peace and comfort when I am weary and on my way home. Hopkins says about our interference with nature, "Even where we mean to mend her we end her."

Ended, the red glow of captured sunlight in the trunks of my alders. Forever ended; the land now mended for cattle - at the sacrifice of my alders.

"My" alders. What a mockery! Does what I hold in my heart belong to me? It's the most ephemeral of all possessions, so easily

67

stolen, the thief never to blame. These three cattle on that mended land and ended light are part of someone's livelihood. What were "my" alders to him but obstacles to his desired end?

Balancing values is a ticklish matter. If the person who cleared that land for his cattle had known about the important thing I had had till he ended it, would he have tried to make arrangements to satisfy both our needs? Could I have given him something as valuable to him as his cattle if I had shown him alder-held sunlight?

Hopkins ended his poem with an expression of the same sadness and sense of loss I feel about my alders and with keen insight into the extent of that loss as more than his own:

> *After-comers cannot guess the beauty been*
> *Ten or twelve, only ten or twelve*
> *Strokes of havoc unselve*
> *The sweet especial scene,*
> *Rural scene, a rural scene,*
> *Sweet especial rural scene.*

The Pretend Strawberry

The May issue of *Bon Appétit* features a full-page color picture of strawberry napoleons with lemon cream. The June issue has a page-and-a-half spread of creamy tartlets topped with strawberry starlets, criss-crossed ladders of sliced strawberries, and strawberry fans with leafy tops. They all look so-o-o-o good. But the point of a fruit is not how it looks or what pretty designs it makes but HOW IT TASTES. And I love strawberries. They are sweet and juicy and richly red, like June sunshine. Their aroma sends saliva sluicing around my mouth. Notice that I did not say I love strawberries because they are big. Nevertheless, the main if not the only virtue of this year's strawberries is that they are big. It's not their sweetness, not their nostril-widening, titillating aroma, not their finger-sticky, red juiciness but their size that attracts. But gigantism does not equal superiority in fruit. This year's strawberries pretend to be strawberries but lack the character of real strawberries. They smell and look like strawberries, but what looks like a skunk and smells like a skunk ain't necessarily a skunk.

Some not so bright strawberry manufacturer must have thought that if strawberries were bigger and lasted longer in the basket, the merchants would like them better. And that's probably true. The strawberry farmers probably love these strawberries. They are easier to pick because they are bigger, and so the picker moves faster, wastes less, and saves the grower money. Picker and grower are happy. The strawberries, being bigger, bruise less easily and mold less quickly. Growers and super market buyers are happy. Since they last longer, these strawberries can be shipped more easily, so distributors are happy, too. Because they are red like strawberries and hold their shape so well - they aren't tender and bruisingly sensitive to the touch - food photographers like them. *Bon Appétit* likes them because their luscious pictures sell magazines. So the strawberry industry flourishes; money turns hands; smiles enlighten faces. Everybody's happy.

Except me. I'm not happy.

Who ever decided that big was better than good? Why would anyone want to substitute shelf life for taste? Not me. I want my little, dark red, deeply tasteful, ambrosia-sweet, old fashioned, temperamental strawberries back on my table again.

Poison Oak Serpent

On a walk down an old logging road through the forest last week, I came to a large puddle blocking my way. On one side, it nestled against two fir trunks, around which wound the long, snaky, mean-eyed limbs of poison oak, waving over the puddle like a nest of serpents. On the other side poison oak grew in a thick·hedge, but between the muddy edge of the puddle and the perilous edge of the thicket, the poison oak branches stretched upward, not out, so that if I leaned away from them I might be able to get by - except for one curvy, snaky, many-angled branch leaning over the puddle like a policeman's gloved hand - or an "access forbidden" sign - or a coiled rattlesnake. If I could develop a strategy for getting past this barricade, I would have a chance, on this side, for continuing my walk.

If the poison oak branch were a traffic cop, I could wait for my turn to pass, but that was a useless approach here. If it were a sign, I could ignore it, if I wanted to, or get permission to pass, but neither approach was applicable in this case. If it were a rattlesnake, I could find a forked stick, catch the neck of the snake in the fork of that stick, and, letting the rattles whir their useless fury, hold the snake down till I was well past the gaping fangs and could jump out of reach of the coil-released snake. At least, that's the way I've heard snakes can be held down. Just because I have never done it before doesn't mean I can't.

I hunted through the woods till I found a sturdy stick with a long fork at the end. The poison oak was eyeing me suspiciously, coiled, ready to strike, rattling with a low, warning buzz. Anticipating a contest of might and cunning, I approached cautiously, and, moving slowly, caught the snaky vines carefully around the throat in the fork of my stick.

That's when the fiend struck. With its rattles booming like war drums, it lashed out with several Hydra arms; I had not one snake but a whole Medusa head going after me. I felt a thump as one of the reptilian limbs slashed me on top of the head - as harmlessly, though, as rattlesnake fangs on a boot, since I was wearing a hat. Struggling for control, I pushed harder against the monster, which was not only exerting strength against my stick but writhing in a vigorous dance that would have made St. Vitus look stationary. I pushed towards the woods and leaned back towards the puddle, holding the brute at bay; I took one step, then another; I passed the baton from my right hand to my left, then made a frantic leap over the tip of the puddle, dropping my stick and springing, I hoped, out of reach of the striking serpent.

Trembling, safe, I turned around. The poison oak was waving its arms, snarling, spitting foam, rattling like crazy. I wiped the sweat off my brow and turned my back on the creature to continue my walk, resolutely putting out of my mind, for the time being, that I would have to face the same danger again on the way home.

When God Forgot the Chlorophyll

God was in a frenzy of creation. He only had six days in which to finish the project, and there was so much to do! But deadlines always arrive; the sixth day did come, and God was just finishing up, painting those last-minute thin lines on the wood duck and looking forward to a day of rest, when he saw the mushrooms. "Oh, my God!" he cried. "I forgot the chlorophyll!" But it was too late. Chagrined, God hurriedly bestowed on mushrooms four compensating factors: strength, shape, the use of all other colors than green, and edibility.

Thus it is that mushrooms push up through the earth with iron-fist force, the eponymous metaphor for unstoppable strength and sudden emergence. Nothing stops a mushroom once it begins pushing itself into the dark, damp light of the forest. Sticks, leaves, bark, logs, and stones are shoved aside; vines that would bind anything else are forced to stretch around and twist the shape of but never stop a mushroom, the quintessential "Out of my way; I'm coming through!" emergent. And yet they are so soft. How could anything as delicate and soft as a mushroom, so mushy to the touch, so spongy and fragile, have such strength?

Mushrooms are flat like tabletops or pointed and curved like umbrellas. They are bulbous or convoluted, small as buttons or big as cups, thin as platters or thick as steaks. They are smooth as a manzanita limb, scaly like lizard's skin, bumpy, flaky, or, in the terminology of the mushroom book, covered with warts, a word much too ugly for the delicate flakes and spots of white on the regally scarlet amanita. Large, yellow-brown, flat mushrooms with edges slightly curled look like buttermilk pancakes, which, when they age, look like they've been left too long on the griddle. Mushrooms are freckled, striped, or plain; they whorl with concentric rings or fade their colors with the delicacy of a sound fade-out. They grow singly, in clumps, or in large colonies. The white ones look like scattered eggshells, the brown ones like chocolate wafers, the orange ones like yam skins; a scattering of mushrooms in the woods looks like a turned-over compost heap. They are shiny, wet, dry, slimy, curly, convex, concave, rubbery, slick. They emerge folded like butterfly wings, or they jam a six-inch-wide top through the earth like the head of a nail being pounded from below. They measure from half an inch across to eight inches or more. They have curdled edges or smooth, tree-trunk stems or toothpick stems, under-layers like petticoats or like leaves of the Bible slightly warped with dampness or like sponges from Florida's seas. They have all the floral colors: red, yellow, purple, grey, white, brown, pink, coral, but no matter how bright the hue, the tone is muted with earthiness.

And they are edible - sometimes. Mushrooms are the big gamble of the vegetable kingdom. "Try me" is the tempting message. Just as good as some are to the palate exactly so poisonous are others. Some mushrooms are so good enthusiasts dare the edges of edibility, others so poisonous the unwary can die for having touched them and brought fingers to tongues. Some mushrooms are poisonous to some people in some circumstances. Other people eat the same mushrooms safely with gusto. And even as some delight the tongue and some poison the body, others send the mind on strange journeys, another gamble between sensual delights and mental dangers. Nothing is certain except the gamble. But the inconsistency is understandable. God was rushed.

The Ecological Continuum of the Forest

Like anyone else, I learned in school about the natural recycling of the forests: logs make dirt that feeds the trees that turn into logs to make more dirt to feed more trees, and that's the way the forest grows. I learned it in school, and I learned it in the woods I grew up in. It was common sense to me, a fact of life as obvious as the turning of the earth measured against the rising and setting of the sun.

But just as there was a time when astronomers thought the earth stood still while the sun encircled it, so there seems to have come a time when foresters have forgotten what makes the forest live. I recently attended a presentation for Forest Service personnel and a few conservationist guests by Chris Maser, a researcher with the Bureau of Land Management. His subject was old-growth forests, and his message was that same truth of my childhood: to deprive the forest of any one of its necessary elements is eventually to destroy the forest. To back up this truth of the necessity of the function of each part for the successful functioning of the whole, he quoted a story from Buddha. Buddha? From a man employed by the Bureau of Land Management? My respect for BLM rose an inch or two from its previous low position.

And so for four hours Chris Maser told us how a forest recycles into its ecological continuum, expanding the simplistic knowledge of my childhood. Intellectually delving into the intricate interrelationships of the forest, he connected not only decaying wood to ants and termites but even the tiny parasite that lives inside the termite's stomach to that same Buddha-istic necessity of function. The underground fungi, which grow on the roots of the firs and facilitate their intake of nitrogen, depend on the voles and chipmunks which feed on that fungi to disseminate their spores. Thus the trees, too, depend on the small mammals to which they give shelter and food. The forest is an organism as tightly interconnected as the parts of a body, an ecological continuum which cannot be deprived of any of its parts without harming the whole.

That was Maser's point. "We cannot continue to take, take, take," he told the foresters. "We must learn to think of the life of a tree not only as the 800 years it will stand but as the additional 400 years it will rot and decay." Furthermore, he reminded us, "most of the world's water comes from the forest watersheds. The most important product of the forest is not wood fiber but water." Like Einstein, who told us at the onset of the atomic age that we must now change our modes of thinking, Chris Maser has urged us likewise and for the same urgent reasons to change our thinking about the forest. Drawing on wisdoms as disparate as Buddha and *Alice in Wonderland*, *The Tao of Physics*, and Elizabeth Kubla-Ross, he reminded our foresters of what in the face of economics (formerly called greed) they may have forgotten: what it is that makes the trees a forest.

Living with Nature

Why We Need the Stars

"Planetariums," Jack Eagleson told the audience as we sat in the Medford Senior High Planetarium for his talk on the Hyakutake comet, "will be the star museums of the future," meaning that the proliferation of pollution will extinguish the stars for us so that we can only see them in facsimile as we now see dinosaurs and other more recently extinct creatures only as models.

It was true that I had left home under a sky flooded with stars only to have them fade in the fog of Medford. Nothing had so graphically brought home to me the difference between my sky and the Medford sky, between the rural sky and the city sky - except for the time I had been a month in Atlanta and one night mistook a streetlight for the moon. I knew then I had been too long in the city; it was time to go home.This difference was also made clear in an advertisement for a camping trip to the eastern Oregon desert. How long has it been, the blurb asked the reader, since you saw the Milky Way? Why, only last night, I laughed, but it was sobering to know that for some the luminous band of celestial light isn't so easily viewed.

Jack told us about the director of a planetarium in Philadelphia who once filled his sky with all the stars visible to the naked eye - 3000 of them; then he blotted out all except those visible in Philadelphia, leaving only 840 stars. Were my thousands of stars still visible at home? I wanted to run home and count them. Maybe Saint-Exupéry's serious businessman who counted stars wasn't as ridiculous as the Little Prince had thought him. It is a terrible thing to lose the stars.

"And with all these stars above you," Jack was saying, "these millions of miles of distances, how can you place yourself, miniscule as you are, in this universe?" Astronomy is humbling, reducing one, as geology does, to one's insignificance. When geologists can speak of the Precambrian time as being four thousand million years ago and that there are 76 million years in the Cretaceous Period and fifty million in the Devonion, "one is tempted," John McPhee says, "to condense time, somewhat glibly - to say, for example, that the faulting which lifted up the mountains of the Basin and Range began 'only' eight million years ago. The late Miocene was 'a mere' eight million years ago. That the Rocky Mountains were building seventy million years ago and the Appalachians were folding four hundred million years ago does not impose brevity on eight million years."

To grasp such time references overwhelms the mind and sets it reeling. I live in my life just under a hundred years - a mere hundred years; I live on a few acres on the side of a seven-thousand-foot mountain, a pebble in distances measured by light-years. How pale, how small, how petty I am, we are. What overblown egos we have when we consider our significance in the face of the space and the time given to us by the stars and the rocks.

But it is the human condition not only to be here but to make something, each of us individually, of our being here. "The great mystery," André Malraux says in *La Condition Humaine*, "is not that we should have been thrown down here at random between the profusion of matter and that of the stars; it is that from our very prison we should draw, from our own selves, images powerful enough to deny our nothingness." It is that that makes us reach towards greatness, even here on our puny and petty, tiny planet earth; but lest we form an illusion of the greatness we have created out of our nothingness, we need look at the stars from time to time.

—

Impressionistic Paintings of the Sky

The moonless midnight sky is a black velvet gown, falling voluptuously to the feet of the roulette queen, besprinkled with thousands upon thousands of sequins and rhinestones, sewn onto the heavy soft cloth by the evening seamstress, who envies as she stitches the riches of the queen, envies as she sews the gaudy galore of the roulette queen.

But when I arise long before dawn and stand outside on my Yaknapatawpha lawn to look at the sky, I see a game of jackstones in progress. The floor is the sky and the jacks are the stars; the floor is ebony and the jacks are diamonds, and the player plays not by ones but by millions, and he is on his two millions now and has already thrown that great gleaming ball, the moon, into the air and is just ready to sweep two million stars out of the sky, or diamonds off the ebony, into his mighty hand. Has he passed lazy Marys, into-the-garage, over-the-fence? Is the game already at the around-the-world stage? Looking at the jacks, I cannot see the ball. I study the throw. Is it a good throw for two millions? Will he set the jack spinning and lose his turn? Will he miss the ball? May I play, too?

The childish moon sets tonight like a child going to bed, with a halo of innocence like that of a Renaissance baby Jesus, a da Vinci Christ child settling his chubby baby's head into the Virgin Mary's motherly lap.

If clouds were roses this earliest sunset cloud would be named Peaches 'n Cream. If they were apples, it would be the lightest blush on a Golden Delicious, and if they were children, this one would be a twelve-year-old girl poised on the threshold for her first dance. Peaches 'n Cream is the grand blue-ribbon winner from the hybrid tea category in the state-wide rose show. The apple I will eat till it vanishes. The little girl blushes more deeply, dances, and is gone. Clouds wisp and dissolve, so roses, apples, girls - *sic gloria mundi transit.*

81

This cloud is as soft as the fuzz on a peach.

The tiniest new moon is a boat for angels to sail across the sky. They alight on the mountain of the western shore, where they tumble from trees to play with dryads. It is a tiara for Mozart's Queen of the Night to wear on opening night of *The Magic Flute*. She plays her part, she takes center stage, she sings her beautiful aria to an audience of angels in the theater of stars, and she glides grandly across the stage to disappear behind the western wings.

The next night a cuckolded Malevio shows his face, wearing his horns, and at the laughing ridicule of his friends and the song of the cuckoo, he hides in shame behind the mountain. Tu-whit, tu-who, and the moon goes down.

Performing Magic with Rocks

A child came to me where I sat on the rocky beach of the swimming hole. She held out her hand, palm up, to show me a pretty green-speckled rock.

"Beth!" I cried in great excitement. "Do you know what you have found? This is a petrified dinosaur's egg. The Great Speckled Dinosaur that lived in the Applegate - you have found its egg!"

Beth knew there was no real truth in what I said, but somehow it seemed full of a magical truth. And if she could believe it, if for only a moment she could believe it, it would be so wonderful! Another child stuck out her hand. In it was a pretty, little, round, clear, white stone.

"Oh, Laurel," I said, impressed. "This is very special, very rare. This is a teardrop of the moon." I spoke solemnly, emphasizing the momentousness of the find.

Suddenly a dozen children were before me, each with a special rock. Who knew who they were and where they came from? And they all wanted me to reveal the stories of their rocks.

"This - oh, my god, look what you have found! A Roman coin, two centuries old. All the way from Italy, all the way across the Atlantic and through the Hudson River and -" That I couldn't trace the watery path of this coin from ancient Rome through the northwest passage to the Applegate River didn't matter. This child had no idea where Rome was or the Hudson River, but the enchantment was as powerful as if the story had been understandable and true.

"And this - Sabrah, you have found the stone door that opens the elves' cave. All you have to do now is find the cave, put the door in place, and then if you knew the magic words, you could get into the cave.... Oh, Colby, how special...."

On and on and on it went. I began to panic as the magic grew until it threatened, as most magic will, to get out of hand. Was my imagination equal to this task? Round rocks, square rocks, red ones, white ones, gray, black, green, or blue ones, crooked rocks, rough rocks, smooth rocks - could I find in the peculiarity of each rock a story, an enchantment? Could I make each one a special, wonderful find, each a piece of magic?

I changed tone rapidly. Excitedly, I told Colby her rock was a find of great significance which the Smithsonian Institute would pay thousands of dollars for. With a tone of great awe, I looked at another child and said, "You are the only person to have found the toenail of the giant wulu bird that inhabited Mount Mazama before it turned inside out and became Crater Lake." My voice was restricted with fear and ominous with warning as I told another child that she had found the tooth of the witch of the Siskiyous, very dangerous, full of poison, best to throw it away.

The spell continued until parents came to take children away, but even then the magic lingered as children chattered excitedly to parents and siblings about their finds, still full of the wonder of their belief, or of their suspension of disbelief. As for me - well, all special moments that work their way into the heart last for a long, long time.

A Musical Evocation
of Air, Fire, Water, and Earth

Sitting on a bench tucked under the fragrant thickets and bushes on a steep hillside overlooking the ocean, I played my guitar. The openness of the air, the distances, the exquisite mystery of ocean and sky said, "Romantics," and so my guitar sang Schumann's "Romanza" and a Chopin prelude. The turquoise ocean with its distant surf matched rhythm for rhythm the soul-expressive tempo, and from far, far away, responding from just over the curve of the earth, a clear, faint song drifted through the sea-fresh air: old Triton blowing his wreathed horn.

In June the ocean, in July the redwoods. Masters of silence, custodians of God's time, keepers of the ancient wisdom, how would the redwoods receive the timid notes of my rosewood guitar? Might they lean over, listen, whisper to each other, "What is this missive that comes to us from one of our own?" It was Bach that belonged in this cathedral where spirit, that fire of the soul, slipped around the trunks and through the long ferns, Bach, the God-inspired, the supplicant to God, the worshiper. The trunks of the redwoods took in the notes of the guitar like pipes of an organ. They absorbed, breathed in the sound, then breathed it out again in soft echo. Here was Bach set free to walk with God in his cathedral again.

In September, the mountain. On top of a five-thousand-foot peak in the Smoky Mountains, where ridges rippled like waves of the ocean and rhythms of music, mists rolled and twirled, kissing the mountaintop. With unrestrained vigor, trees, vines, bushes, and shrubs, fed by rains and mists, fought and elbowed each other in a wild rampage to reach the top of the mountain. There, abruptly, all were turned back by the magic spell of the gardener. Flowers of the darkest blues and most startling reds and yellows flounced at the edges of a lake-green lawn; nooks of succulents crawled into rock walls; arches of twisted vines and trunks framed distant mountains; cool waters tumbled over rock fountains. In the center of the garden, with the reach of an obelisk and the loveliness of a gem, stood a fairy-tale house of unblemished glass and polished wood, maroon and white tile floors, red-blond window sills. Inside the house, dry by the window and warm by the fireplace, I sent from my guitar into the water-kissed landscape the soft, rippling arpeggio beauty of Ferdinand Sor, echoing the arpeggios of mountains and arpeggios of mists.

Later in September, the hollows of the earth. Deep underground, in the Ghost Room of Oregon Caves, when the electric lights were turned off, dark was as thick and unrelenting as syrup, the smell of earth damp and pungent, the air heavy, clammy, and cool, and the ear alert, witness to the drip of water building stalactite temples century by century, to the earthy hollowness that was itself a sound, and then, increasingly, to the rich, deep tone of my shakuhachi flute, a tone rooted in earth like the bamboo it came from, a sound that grew in volume till it flowed through the cave big and round, like rivers and wind, like rooms in a cave, like Gollum's secret. The ghosts of earth glided out of hiding and hung with the music, until the last single, solemn, rich note of bamboo floated into the black emptiness. Then the emptiness hung there alone. It was time to crawl out of the belly of the whale.

The Price Exacted for Essential Nourishment

For several months a friend of mine was coming to see me once a week. I'm very fond of him, and he of me, so we both enjoyed these visits. I cooked Tom good things to eat, and he always did the nicest things around the house - replumbed the shower, fixed the kitchen faucet, replaced the stovepipe.

Then one day, in an outburst of vexation, sorrow, and honesty, he said he wouldn't be coming up here once a week any more. The drive, he said, was too much. It was just too far, he said. If I lived next door to him, he said, he would be over every day, but I live way up the mountain on a steep gravel road his truck detests and up a steep hill he doesn't much like to climb himself, and he has children he wants to be home for and other obligations in his daily life, and it was altogether just too much. He promised to stay in touch and drove away, leaving me standing on the road wondering when we would see each other again and a little melancholy at that vacancy he was leaving in the middle of my week.

The next day I drove to the town of Rogue River to help a friend with a book she is writing, and I thought about what Tom had said the whole time I was driving there because Lenor seemed to live awfully far away. (Only it is I, of course, who live far away.) And I remembered last spring, when I was part of a writers' salon that met at Lenor's house once a week and how, after a few months, I knew that I could not keep it up. It was too much. It was too far. The drive was too long. Tom was right.

A man once told me, years ago, that I was "geographically undesirable." At the time I thought it was a funny phrase (he was undesirable himself for other reasons) and that he was speaking only for himself. Now I'm wondering. I'm looking at my life from Tom's perspective, and I'm wondering if maybe I pay a heavy price for this home I love so much. It doesn't seem to me that I live so remotely, partly because I know it's only luck that I didn't end up living even more isolated than I do, and partly because my life is full of activity and friends I love and work I find fulfilling, and partly because I make the drive into the valley twice a week to teach at the college, and it doesn't seem so far when I do it. But driving down the mountain into the valley, where so many people live among so much activity, takes isolation and moves it to community, which shortens distance, whereas doing it the other way around lengthens distance. It was not only the time it took to drive to my house but the concept of driving into isolation that made the distance seem so far to Tom.

Tom appreciates my home, but he said he could never live up here, being, as he says, a "city boy." I claimed I could never live in town, either, but he refuted that. And maybe I could, but I know that if I did, a little part of me would die. And that little part of me that needs and loves and holds to the natural world in its wilder spirit is the part I pay a heavy price to keep alive. But I wouldn't be the same person Tom knows now if I lived next door to him. Perhaps more than most people, I am molded and sculpted by my environment. Those are fortunate who have learned what it is that feeds their souls. And once we do, we know that we will pay the price exacted for that essential nourishment.

Getting to the Root of the Matter

The road that passes in front of my house is a deeply rutted, unmaintained, dirt road, more suitable for feet than for cars. At a certain place in this road, an unusual root formation rises to the surface in a perfect X, in the center of which, at the crossing of the lines, the roots sink back into the ground in a space just big enough for a foot. For years whenever I walked the road, some vague superstitious nature of my ancestors would rise to the fore at that root to prevent me from stepping in that crossing. Finally, though, I passed that way and thought, "How silly. Who's to say that stepping in this rooted X would bring me misfortune? Maybe it would bring me good luck. And, anyway, a root is a root. Superstition, begone!" and I boldly stepped right in the middle of the X, in the space just big enough for a foot.

Nothing happened, of course. Elves and leprechauns didn't jump angrily out of the woods, nor, for that matter, did fairies appear to grant me three wishes. I arrived at the house of my friend and spent a pleasant afternoon, but about an hour before I was to start for home, my foot began to hurt. It was a slow, building ache with no apparent cause. I had a mile to walk home and was vaguely uneasy, so I left immediately, but even before I started the walk, I was limping. Would I have to limp all the way home? What else to do? I was anxious to get home; the ache in my foot was dominating all thought - except, of course, I was thinking about the root. I hobbled fast, but a mile is a mile.

At last I reached home and did the necessary chores in a daze, then climbed the ladder to my bedroom loft and crawled into bed with relief. There I concentrated on the pain in my foot. The ache was intense. I examined the foot and found no wound, no puncture. The source of the ache seemed to be in the heel, but I could find no mark there. I lay in bed wondering what I should do. I didn't have a telephone; should I hobble to my neighbor's and have her take me to the doctor? The last thing I wanted to do was walk on that foot again. Poultices or mustard plasters? The last thing I wanted to do was get out of bed and climb down the ladder on that foot again.

The moon rose over the mountain, tucked itself behind the forest, and then slipped from behind the madrone tree to shine into my skylight full, round, brilliant, and far away. "Ow! My foot is killing me!" I thought, and then I thought in alarm, "What if it really is?" Blood poisoning? Bone cancer? Slowly, steadily, the moon turned black. Eclipsed by the shadow of the earth, the light of the moon dimmed and went out until it was only a dull glow behind the blackness of the shadow; then, slowly, steadily the moon slipped out from behind the shadow until it was its full, brilliant roundness again. At that point, it disappeared behind the western madrone, and I could see it no longer. I fell asleep with the ache in my foot and the eclipse of the moon winding themselves into my unconscious mind.

The next morning the ache was gone; the foot had returned to normal, and my mind could think of other things. I never did know the source of the pain that eclipsed my mind that night. Those who like to think it is the earth's shadow that covers the light of the moon will rest their minds with an explanation of a spider bite or a delayed reaction to the scorpion sting I had suffered a day before. But those who agree with Albert Einstein that "the most beautiful thing we can experience is the mysterious....He to whom this emotion is a stranger, who can no longer pause to wonder and stand rapt in awe, is as good as dead; his eyes are closed" - they are those who stand in awe of eclipses as of root formations. They leave room for doubt, for wonder, for elves, leprechauns, and fairies. But perhaps there are those who, like me, throw out superstition with the acquisition of understanding but retain the wonder. They, too - and not for superstition - will never step into the center of the root again.

Witchery

Stealthily I look over my shoulder down the unused road. Not a soul in sight, up the road or down. Surreptitiously, cautious as a deer, I step to the edge of the woods and begin picking St. John's wort blossoms. Quickly I pluck them off their stalks and into my bag. No one is likely to saunter by, but you never can tell - and you can't be too careful. One must always be wary of bigoted eyes and ears. At last I have two double handfuls of little yellow blossoms, and I head home, my reapings concealed in the pack on my back. Home, I put them in a jar (just an old mayonnaise jar; I'm not an apparatus-meticulous witch), cover them with oil, and set them in the sun. After shaking them daily for two weeks, I strain my St. John's wort oil, cap it tightly, and store it in a cool, dry place, a medicine for stopping bleeding.

Women have been burned at the stake for such as that. It wasn't their knowledge of herbs and medicines that led to their deaths but the fear-ridden vision of bigoted neighbors. "Men feared witches and burned women." Am I safe from those eyes? There were those who saw me shake my jar of reddening oil. I'm not really afraid of accusations of witchcraft, but neither did I advertise my witch's art: "Excuse me while I shake my potion" - no. Nor do I show all my visitors the red clover and the yarrow flowers drying under the heat of the roof or offer them a plantain leaf if they cut a finger. I don't like to be laughed at any more than I like to be feared. Derision is a hot fire.

But, really, what is a witch? On the one hand, an ugly old woman, a hag; on the other, a bewitching, charming young girl. Chinese is not the only language in which intonation conveys meaning, and although English is supposedly not one, I'll know which witch you mean if you call me witch.

When did the charming young girl turn into the old hag? We want to be bewitching, to use our bewitchery for power with a certain susceptible somebody. To that end we apply our violet-and-goat's milk concoction to our complexions and tramp the hillsides for bedstraw which, when mixed with mutton broth, is supposed to make the figure slim. (Laura Martin, author of *Wildflower Folklore*, says it's the tramping and not the broth that makes the figure youthful. Jogging is the modern witch's bedstraw broth.)

In *Henry VI*, Shakespeare's Richard says, "I'll witch sweet ladies with my words and looks." So would we our men. Why is it, then, that when we try our enchantments, we hear, "Aroint thee, witch"? We put forth to please; our aim goes awry. From the enchanting young sorceress with powers of healing the heart (or breaking the heart), we become, through no act of our own, only through the bigoted eyes of our gentleman friends, crones and hags. What was once a deliciously enticing making of magic has become the suspicious meddling of the old gossip: "Foul, wrinkled witch, what makest thou in my sight?" Foul, suspicious sir, nought that I would serve to you, for my magic is for those who would see my witchery with other eyes.

The healer's power and the charmer's power belong to the witches, and perhaps men justly fear them. But they are wrong to burn us, for our witchery is their fountain of youth.

> *When have I last looked on*
> *The round green eyes and the long wavering bodies*
> *Of the dark leopards of the moon? [Yeats writes]*
> *All the wild witches, those most noble ladies,*
> *For all their broom-sticks and their tears,*
> *Their angry tears, are gone.*
> *The holy centaurs of the hills are vanished;*
> *I have nothing but the embittered sun;*
> *Banished heroic mother moon and vanished,*
> *And now that I have come to fifty years*
> *I must endure the timid sun.*

Well, then, Yeats and ye others, bring back "all the wild witches, those most noble ladies."

Trapped in Williston Barrett

What a winter this has been! Record cold in November with Laplander-style ice and snow, followed by a month of Florida-style sunshine. December was so pleasant, in fact, I began to worry. Ursula LeGuin's Earthsea proverb droned in my ear: "Rain on Roke may be drouth in Osskils, and a calm in the East Reach may be storm and ruin in the West." Here, a rainless winter means drought in the summer. No rain here at home means no snowcap on Greyback Mountain means no water in July. I became afflicted with the symptom of backwardness of Williston Barrett, the "last gentleman" of Walker Percy's novel by that name, a mild gentlemanly Southerner, slightly amnesiac, who couldn't get things straight. When other people felt good, he felt bad, and when they felt bad, he felt good. So with me. Why couldn't I just enjoy the weather? Why did I have to worry about drought in the future? Good old Taoistic Pooh wouldn't have fretted. I was being an Eeyore, and doleful Eeyores not only never have fun; they never do any good, either.

Suddenly, my worry notwithstanding, rains came, and when they came, they rolled in with a vengeance against drought. Creeks and rivers swelled to the breaking point, and the talk was not of too little water but of too much. True to Williston Barrett's symptoms, however, I felt good while others felt bad, rejoiced while others worried. Was I concerned about floods? No, not I. I thrilled too much to the power of the water, to the ungovernable force of the rivers high and rich and full.

Then the rains stopped, and the creeks and rivers returned to normal, but the abnormalities of the winter weren't over yet. Next we had record-breaking warmth, and premature spring popped out everywhere. My plum tree, starting at the top where the branches reach closest to the sun, peeped out, saw that the weather was good, and continued dressing its winter nakedness in frothy blossoms. But I held true to Williston Barrett. While everyone else was feeling good in the sudden spring, I was feeling bad. I was alarmed. "No, no, no!" I cried to my plum tree. "Too early! Too early!" I wanted to force blossoms back into buds, to lull each little white eye asleep again. "Don't you know it's only the end of February, poor little things?" I sobbed.

And then the rains returned and the wind, and with a shudder my plum tree shed all its foamy blossoms. Like a girl whose petticoat has slipped to her feet, it stands in its embarrassment, knowing there will be no plums in August. But in the woods the spring rains have urged awake the fawn lilies, the grouse-flower, and the shooting stars. Woolly lambs bound across the meadows, and my lawn grows lushly to the cutting point. I can't control the too-early blossoming of fruit trees any more than I can the floods of the rivers, so why should I deprive myself of enjoying spring in March just because I won't be able to enjoy plums in August? With the effort of breaking bonds, I abandon Williston Barrett.

Ah! Much better. I feel in step again, not with the attitudes of other people but with the way things are. Pooh-like, I enjoy life. Pirsig-like, I move through life, taking my cue not from the hero of *The Last Gentleman*, but from the author of *Zen and the Art of Motorcycle Maintenance*, Robert Pirsig, who, riding his motorcycle with friends through the emptiness of Kansas, said, "I don't want to own these prairies, or photograph them, or change them, or even stop or even keep going. We are just moving down the empty road."

Reflections on Pain

Pain shattered starlike from my shin. The center pulsated with hot yellow rays; the horizontal starburst shot in all directions, fading into space before reaching the ankle or the knee. The splintering pain indicated splintered bones, falsely, of course; I wouldn't be able to walk on my leg if it were broken. I clung to the fact. I limped across the dark of the lawn to the path to the outhouse, moaning aloud, then limped back to the doorway of the house where I pulled myself inside by climbing the stump the board had lain on, the board which hit my shin as it flew off its stump legs as I stepped on it to go outside this dark and starry winter night.

The next day as I sat at my desk writing, I noticed a little stinging insect on my left, a red-tailed, winged, lady-like-looking little bug. Speak softly but carry a big stick. She seems innocuous, but her sting is vicious. She had stung me a year or so ago; only a month before, she had dropped into my son's bed and stung him on the ear, giving him a painful awakening. I looked at her and remembered, and with a swift apology and vengeful courtesy, I smashed her with two quick slaps of my hand into the paper on the desk.

Gore oozed out of her stinging end. Her delicate wings half-lifted from the paper, and her two long antennae curled gracefully high above her prominent eyes. Her legs waved, climbing the air, trying to pull the body back into life, but the body, stuck tightly to the paper by the body's goo at the stinging end, refused to follow. The stinging end. Poor little lady, had you not had this stinging end, you would not have met this violent end. Live by the sword, die by the sword. But didn't I last night endure pain, too? Is mine greater because I am proportionately bigger? Or is yours greater because you are proportionately smaller? Or is yours greater because it is your death agony? Or is mine greater because I am of a higher consciousness?

Shameful words! Of a higher consciousness? It was I who killed the innocent fairy bug with its stinging end. Don't we all have a stinging end? What if I were struck down every time I stung a fellow being? - or even whenever a fellow being looked at me, remembered the sting of another of my kind, and slapped me to the paper for it? If I saw that stuff that oozed out of my stinging end, would I claw the air for clemency?

With the grace of a charging steed, each portion of the body perfectly, architecturally placed, the little red insect relinquished her spirit, and, freed from her pain, gained the Elysian Fields. I, pitiful, lumbering beast of humankind, shouldered my painful burden and limped into my destiny.

A Lunch Just This Side of Heaven

For a lunch so exquisite you could share it with visiting angels, try apples, cheese, and dates. Not just any old apple, cheese, and dates will do, of course; as with all good meals, the excellence is in the ingredients.

Begin with a good apple, a Golden Delicious you have just plucked off the tree. It should be light green, almost yellow-green on one side with maybe the barest blush of pink at a highlighted edge, where the neighboring plum tree left a kiss. Don't try to substitute a super market apple. The results will be disappointing.

Slice the apple cleanly in half with one swift curve of your knife. It will crack open with a crisp snap, revealing flesh as white as whipped cream, as hard as walnuts, as glistening wet as a glass of cold beer. Cut each half into half again, core each quarter, and cut it in half. The apple will sweat gently into your palm.

Put the eight pieces of apple on your favorite plate, bunching them to leave room for the cheese and dates.

Choose a strong, sharp cheese. Emmenthaler has the best tongue-biting sharpness; a good, sharp cheddar is also suitable. Don't try mild cheeses like Monterey Jack or Gouda; they are too bland. Don't try feta; it's too salty, and don't use cream cheeses; they are too soft and not sharp enough. The only substitute for a good sharp cheese is tahini, which, like cheese, has a strong enough taste to contrast with the dates and apple. Cut four pieces of cheese, fingerlength, and lay them on the plate with the apple slices.

Put six dates on the plate with the apples and cheese. Deglect noirs are best. The candy-like medjools are good, but too expensive They're too rich to eat every day, anyway, like a surfeit of parties. Raisins or other dried fruit can be substituted for dates, but they reduce the quality of the experience. Dates, really.

Take a bite of apple, sweet with autumn sap and cold nights. Ideally you would have waited till after the first frost for this lunch or at least till the nights have offered a touch of cold to sharpen the apple's sweetness and firm its flesh, to give it a perkiness, like a saucy rhyme or a feather in a cap. With the bite of apple still in your mouth, take a bite of cheese. Let the sting of the cheese meet the sweetness of the apple. Let the soft texture of the cheese melt over the hard pieces of apple in the warmth of your mouth. The cheese lasts a bit longer than the apple, so take another bite of apple; then put a date in your mouth. Dark, subtle, teasing, like exotic, belly-dancing Muslims, the honeyed sweetness of the date offsets the tart sweetness of the apple, which is commanding and brilliant. Yang and yin entwine and become one as you chew. The two kinds of sweet mingle and marry; they swirl in clouds of taste in your mouth.

Vary the pattern from time to time by trying date and cheese without apple. The similarity of textures soon cries out for apple, but the tastes, the combination of sour-sharp cheese and rich-sweet date, are exquisite together, at least for a few minutes. The ultimate, really, is to hold the three tastes - apple, date, cheese - in combination but separately; like mixing paints, the optimum beauty is the three colors swirling together just before the inevitable - and ultimately desired - blend: the creamy light yellow of natural cheese, the white of fresh apple, and the black of good dates; the soft cheese, the crunchy apple, the chewy dates.

Even as you started with apple, end with apple. This last bite will cleanse your palate and leave your tongue refreshed, just as the apple, dates, and cheese have delighted your stomach and vaulted your sense of taste to heaven.

If angels are dining with you, don't forget to double the proportions.

Lithia's Meneheunes

One lovely late-summer day I filled a picnic basket with sandwiches and fruit and met my friend Rod in Ashland for lunch. He suggested we eat at a quiet spot at the top of Lithia Park where we wouldn't be bothered by crowds, a charming niche in the woods along the creek's bend. Once there, I chose for our table the flat sun-warmed rock in the middle of the creek. We rock-hopped to it, took off our shoes to dandle our feet in the water, and spread our lunch. Just as I bit into my sandwich, we were attacked.

Like a swarm of insects little children poured over the top of the hill, down to the creek, and into the water. Like bees who know where the nectar is they made for the pool below us. Like lemmings, stopping for nothing, they clambered over our rock and into the sea below. Repeated cycles multiplied their numbers. As though we were a *fata Morgana*, as though the mists of Avalon had closed over us, we became invisible and inaudible; my laughter, though loud in my ears, had no effect on the children. One held to my arm for support as he climbed onto our rock. Something about my flesh must have felt strange to him, not quite like stone, because for a moment he looked at me funny; then, dismissing me as both incomprehensible and non-consequential, he jumped off the rock and into the pool below.

I once saw my father hold a swarm of bees on his out-stretched arm. They buzzed and crawled with never-ceasing activity, seemingly unaware of the human being they crawled over and around. So it was with the children. "There have only been a few times in my life," Rod commented from the midst of the swarm, "when I have been so still in the woods that the wildlife has come unafraid around me."

"This is different," I said. "You don't have to be still. They don't even know we're here."

By this time the mothers in charge of the birthday party - as I surmised it was by the balloons on the bank - were concerned at our plight. They called the children back, but the children paid no attention.

99

"Have you ever noticed," Rod said, ever the scientific observer, "how water renders children deaf? Never mind!" he called back to the perplexed mothers, who really didn't know what to do. "They're not bothering us."

I couldn't stop laughing. At least it was a cinch we weren't bothering them.

"In Hawaii they would be called meneheunes, the little people," Rod said. Maybe in Hawaii. I still called them insects.

Gradually they left. They may have been responding to the calls of the mothers, but I think it more likely they were responding to the natural instinct of insects - I mean, children - to move from one thing to another, from water games to birthday cake. Soon only two or three children were left buzzing around us, the way a few bees remain after you've removed the sweets. Then even they receded and were gone. The birthday party swarmed up the hill, and we were left in peace again.

I took a second bite of my sandwich at last. "You just never can tell," I said, "what sort of creature might descend upon you at a quiet picnic in the woods."

The Saturday In-between

It was after the play, after coffee and cheesecake at Gepetto's, and after midnight; we would take a walk through town and to the park, we decided, before I left Ashland to drive home.

The park was dark and quiet, sweetly scented. Ducks waddled and complained when I walked too close to their sleepy clusters. The pond was black, swimming ducks but cardboard silhouettes; only the two white swans, gracefully curved and shining in the moonlight, were full-bodied and alive. Smoothly and silently they glided, the dark shapes of pond and trees and bushes and clouds around them the essential setting for their beauteous act.

All moments suspended in time are nevertheless but moments in time, and time keeps moving, as so, too, did I have to. It was time and past time to be going home, and so we walked back through town to my car.

A group of teen-age boys loitered on a corner; a snatch of conversation drifted by: "You can tell he's not gay because...." On the next block, white primroses, viciously torn from their flower boxes, were strewn along the sidewalk. Shocked, we gathered the flowers, which, though suffering, were still alive, and replanted them, decrying pernicious vandalism. "It's something I don't understand," we said to each other, shaking our heads, agreeing on how deplorable it was, these flowers ripped from the earth, tossed into the gutter, left dying white in the darkness of hard concrete, as though someone had jerked the swans out of the pond and slit their throats - those graceful white swans swimming in the dark at Lithia Park.

The day before, in Grants Pass, while walking to the laundromat, I passed a parked car with two little girls in it, twins, crying for Mama. The news has been full of abducted children lately, so, not wanting to alarm the mother, I started to walk by and keep out of what wasn't my business anyway. But I can't callously ignore a crying child any more than I can step over desecrated flowers. I stopped and spoke to the girls through the open car window. "Don't worry. Your mother will be right back. She just went into that shop, just for a minute." Indeed, the mother came hurrying at once out of the store.

101

Had she finished her errand? Or had I scared her by my kindness? As I shouldered my laundry and went on my way, I shouldered as well the burden of a people who cannot trust the kindness of a stranger.

I remembered, too, an episode from my childhood when I was on the other side of that conflict. I was running to catch a bus in downtown Atlanta, worried that I would miss it and not meet my mother on time. I must have looked scared to death, for a man stopped me and asked if something was wrong and if he could help me. That scared me even more; I wasn't supposed to talk to strangers, but, in fact, as I realize now, I only took him for the stranger he thought I was running from. He wanted to help me; my refusal left him helpless to be kind, shouldered on him the same burden of a people who can't trust the kindness of a stranger. Would he stop the next time to offer his help?

Although it's true that children are abducted, it's also true that strangers can be kind, and kind strangers should be trusted. I don't want to forget the beauty of the moonlit swans when I come upon the uprooted primroses. What if the tale had ended with Good Friday? No, there is an Easter, and if yesterday was Good Friday, tomorrow is Easter. But today is Saturday, the day in-between.

Leaf Blowers on Trial

It's a beautiful autumn day on the Rogue Community College campus. RRRRRRRR! The oaks are dropping their golden yellow leaves, the sweet gums their tricolored pages. RRRRRRR! But there are no leaves on the ground. RRRRRRRR! The awesome leaf blower, roaring and menacing, huffing and puffing, bellowing and blowing, has turned its snout on every leaf and blown it to kingdom come. RRRRRRRR!

I'll see you in court, leaf blower! I'll put you behind bars, where you belong!

Prosecution: The leaf blower pollutes. It belches exhaust and noise like a nineteenth century train. It roars past my office like a diesel truck on I-5. I can't hear the leaves snap from their twigs, can't listen to them tumbling to earth.

Defense: The leaf blower is efficient.

Prosecution: Contrast the rake. A rake connects the user with the rich smell of composting leaves and damp earth under leaves. The raker has a sense of earth, of cycles and seasons, of smells and sounds. The leaf blower says, "Don't breathe"; the rake says, "Breathe." The leaf blower says, "Don't listen"; the rake says, "Listen." The scrape of the rake over the grass is subtle and small, an irregular monotony like the scratching of chickadees looking for seeds. Would you have students listen to the Zen master in the rake or the tyrant in the leaf blower?

Defense: Leaf blowers do the job.

Prosecution: Why do we need to blow the leaves off the parking lot? Will autumn leaves dirty our car tires? Why can't we kick through leaves on the sidewalks? Why can't the leaves lie where they fall? Why not let us hear again the gentle fluttering of light butterfly leaves scuffed by a breeze? Why can't we know the smell of must and dust, the slight stink of wet leaves moldering on concrete sidewalks? What's wrong with all that that we have to delete it from our autumn experience?

Defense: The leaf blower costs less in labor hours.

Prosecution: Are you sure? Leaf blowers are voraciously ambitious. In autumn there are leaves, in winter, puddles. RRRRRRRR! Blow those puddles to smithereens! Don't, for goodness sake, make us walk around puddles. RRRRRRR! Is it really a good use of the time of our maintenance department to blow water off the sidewalks in a winter rain?

Defense: Leaf blowers do a necessary job.

Prosecution: Okay. Let's say I give you that there is reason sometimes to get leaves off the sidewalk. You could use a rake, but we'll let that go. Let's say I even give you that it's easier to walk on a sidewalk without having to jump puddles. (Brooms work, too, for sweeping water, but we'll let that go, too.) Consider the following story as one last damning indictment against leaf blowers.

It was a lovely spring day on the Rogue Community College campus. Apple-cheeked clouds floated in the bluebell sky. The crabapple tree puffed out its pink-blossom cheeks. As I walked to class I breathed deeply of warm-as-pie-out-of-the-oven spring air. And then - RRRRRRRR! A leaf blower!? But why? This was spring - the time of the singing of birds (RRRRRRRRR!) - the gentle breezes (RRRRRRRR!). The leaf blower hove into sight, bellowing its stinky breath, snuffling after - blossoms! Tiny, sweet, pink blossoms dotting the sidewalk like snowdrops, like freckles on a young girl's cheeks, like raisins in apple pie, like all things pied and piebald and dappled. "Praise God for dappled things!" cried Hopkins, but we - when we see spots on asphalt, we have to get them off. Get those blossoms off! Damn blossoms! Out, damn spots! As though the beautiful spring blossoms are blots of crime. Will we next be trying to blow even the dappled shadows of the trees themselves off the sidewalk?

Your honor, I rest my case.

Rough and Ready Word Journeys

Last month, as participant in a writing workshop led by author David Rains Wallace, I went on several hikes along Rough and Ready Creek in the Siskiyou Mountains. On one of these, Wallace suggested that writers should not stop at the word itself but journey into the word. Consequently, that day, I took the following journeys:

Fir is fir (dead end - no journey), and cedar is cedar (another dead end), but with pine I can travel, as pine comes from Latin *opimus*, which means fat, and so in pine we find pine nuts rich in fat, and resin that burns like fat and oozes like grease, which comes from Latin *crassus*, another word for fat, and so if we follow the etymological association, consonant transference, and rhyme - *opimus* to *crassus*, greases to grasses - the pine tree becomes a kind of grass.

Serpentine soil is named for serpentine rock, which is named for the serpent whose patterned back the rock resembles, the serpent who was named for the Sanskrit "one who crawls." Serpentine rock, therefore, is a rock that crawls, and serpentine soil, as I could see by looking where I was standing, is one that crawls with rocks.

That the insect-eating *Darlingtonia Californica* is named for Mr. Darlington of California could lead to fascinating tales, but without biographical information, the word is a dead end journey. This same plant is also called the cobra lily, named for the cobra, which it resembles by its hood, and the lily, which it resembles by its flower. As the cobra is a serpent, it is appropriate to find the cobra lily crawling around in serpentine-soil fens looking for insects.

Fen is an Old English word for a swamp-like place, and, indeed, according to David Rains Wallace, Rough and Ready Creek used to be a bald cypress swamp like the Okefenokee in south Georgia, where the insectivorous pitcher plant grows, which is called pitcher plant for the same reason cobra lilies are called cobra lilies (resemblance), which is the same reason the Siskiyous' manzanitas are called manzanitas, or, translated from the Spanish, little (very little) apples. But manzanitas are also called bear berries for a different reason (association: food source for said ursine), which is probably not the reason for the name of Hooker's balsam root. That is to say, balsam root was not a food source for Kerby hookers.

The yellow-legged frog found in a tiny bowl of a pond near Rough and Ready Creek is named for the same reason the strange-headed bug is named (description), and these are not dead-end journeys because one can imagine many wonders for the yellow-legged frog and the strange-headed bug, whereas fir is fir and cedar is cedar, period, end of story. Furthermore, the yellow-legged frog was named for a yellow-legged Sanskrit "one who leaps," and according to the lineage of the strange-headed bug, the Greek *kobalos* (meaning "outright knave") beget the Middle French *gobelin*, which beget the English goblin, which beget the bogey, which beget the bug.

Organisms, says Wallace, are better indicators of antiquity than rocks, the truth of which is attested to by today's journeys. Manzanita is always manzanita (apples are apples), but peridotite rock is one thing here and another thing there, shifting with the mineral content but treacherously, stubbornly retaining the name. On the other hand, serpents and frogs take us as far back as Sanskrit, where we learn that frogs leap and serpents crawl. A journey through pines and grasses takes us to ancient Rome, one through cobra lilies to India, and we go deep into some Spanish past with the name of the giant cats, the jaguars, that, Wallace claims, once lay on the peridotite rock along Rough and Ready Creek, licking their paws.

The Story of an Earring

This story, like all good stories, begins with "once upon a time." Like many good fairy tales, it begins with a party. There was no thirteenth fairy at this party, but there was a treasure, and this treasure, as in many stories, had a certain magic to it, so that in object could be seen place, and to place could be given story.

One day I was invited to a party by friends who were dancers and performers. It was held in a small theatre, and the "party games" were improvisation exercises and creative play. Just as I was jumping onto the stage for one set of improv exercises, a pair of earrings lying at the edge of the stage caught my eye. From a thin, single-wire, silver circle dangled long strings of tiny beads and stones - turquoise, lapis, amethyst, malachite, pink crystals, and long, thin strands of silver. They were so enchanting I picked them up to admire them better, and then, like the girl in the fairy tale who, pretending to be a man so she could prove she was as good as the prince and, being suspected and tested, rode a horse as well as he and shot an arrow as accurately as he but gave herself away when she was left alone in a room full of jewels because she couldn't resist adorning herself, I slipped the earrings into my ears.

"They look better on you than they do on me," someone said, and I looked up at Amy, whose earrings they were. Quickly, guiltily, I took them off, but she said, "You can have them."

My protestations were honest, but not too fervent, lest she take me at my word and retract her gift like the monkey in the Brazilian tale who gave away things only to return later and demand them back, saying, "What?! You ate the cakes? I didn't give you that flour; I only loaned it to you!" But Amy was no monkey; she really did give me her earrings.

They are beautiful and unusual earrings, and I like them for that, but I like them even more, now, for the story they carry with them. Amy herself is entwined with those pretty stones and beads, her spirit and the story of her gift tied as tightly into the dangling colors as though strung on their wires.

And so perhaps I can be forgiven for overreacting when, one day last summer, while I was swimming at the Mars swimming hole near the Illinois River, I pulled myself onto the rocks of the shore and realized I had lost an earring. To lose a pretty thing is a pity, but a small one. After all, material things are but material things, and to practice Buddhist non-attachment is good for the soul, so except for a momentary sigh of regret, perhaps I should have accepted the loss. But either I'm not a very good Buddhist or the spirit of Amy was entreating me from the bottom of Mars not to let her drown full fathom five and have Ariel sing of her bones become coral and her eyes become pearls because, distressed beyond all proportion, I let out a cry of dismay that I had lost an earring.

Responding, I think, more to my tone than to the event itself - but maybe unconsciously responding to the story they didn't know - several of the people with me at the swimming hole immediately searched with their eyes the bottom of the pool, which was clearly visible through twenty feet of transparently clean water.

"I see it!" Mary cried, pointing into the deep, green water and directing my eyes to the silver circle of my earring, gleaming like an underwater, disfocused moon on Mars. Encouraged, I dove in to retrieve my treasure. Three times I dove; three times I slithered along the gravely bottom groping with open fingers and closed eyes (I thought that to lose a contact lens for the sake of a bauble would be foolish, if Amy's spirit will forgive me for that materialistic perspective). Two times I came up for air empty-handed; the third time I dove, my fingers closed around the silver ring, and I pushed off from the bottom with the earring held triumphantly aloft like a treasure retrieved from the sunken Titanic.

Now when I wear these earrings, from my ears dangles not only the spirit of Amy but also the secret green pool of the hard red planet, a blending of the malachite and turquoise colors of my beads. In these stones I feel the sharp rocks of Mars under my feet as I poised to dive. In the pink crystals I smell the azalea-honeyed air I emerged to from a swim. In the dangle of the beads I see the gliding head of a green-and-gray dappled snake swimming ahead of me. In these earrings now is tied as though on wire the sweet cold water of Mars, the tumbling currents of the creek, the blunted boulders of Siskiyou eons, and, beyond, in another world, the snowy peaks of the high Siskiyou Mountains.

Thus it is that things attain value, and not only earrings but places, too. To know a place, I was told by a banquet speaker the night after I almost lost my earring at Mars, one must enter it, recognize it, communicate with it, and fall in love with it. The stories one accrues by knowing a place in this way are the stories one dangles on a silver loop of memory and love and become the means by which we hold such places dear and know them as treasures we don't want to lose. Thomas Berry tells us that to move into the Ecological Age we must change the story on which our civilization is based - no longer the Christian myth that has upheld the Industrial Age but now the great story of creation of the earth and all its natural wonders. Braided into this story of evolution as the great underlying story that will give us the psychic depth necessary for living in the Ecological Age are those other, more personal stories, those by which we know a place, through which we communicate with it, from which we learn to love it. Stories are encased in stories, one within the other like Chinese boxes, like Russian dolls, like beads and stones dangling from the silver loop of an earring.